Standard Grade | Credit

Physics

Credit Level 1998

Credit Level 1999

Credit Level 2000

Credit Level 2001

Credit Level 2002

Credit Level 2003

© Scottish Qualifications Authority

All rights reserved. Copying prohibited. No part of this publication may be reproduced, stored in a retrieval system, or transmitted in any form or by any means, electronic, mechanical, photocopying, recording or otherwise.

First exam published in 1998.
Published by
Leckie & Leckie, 8 Whitehill Terrace, St. Andrews, Scotland KY16 8RN
tel: 01334 475656 fax: 01334 477392
enquiries@leckieandleckie.co.uk www.leckieandleckie.co.uk

Leckie & Leckie Project Team: Peter Dennis; John MacPherson; Bruce Ryan; Andrea Smith

ISBN 1-84372-105-8

A CIP Catalogue record for this book is available from the British Library.

Printed in Scotland by Scotprint.

Leckie & Leckie is a division of Granada Learning Limited, part of Granada plc.

Leckie × Leckie
Scotland's leading educational publishers

Introduction

Dear Student,

This past paper book offers you the perfect opportunity to put into practice what you should know in order to do well in your exams. As these questions have actually appeared in the exam in previous years, you can be sure they reflect the kind of questions you will be asked this summer.

Work carefully through the papers, not only to test your knowledge and understanding but also your ability to handle information and work through more thought-provoking questions. Use the answer booklet at the back of the book to check that you know exactly what the examiner is looking for to gain top marks. You will be able to focus on areas of weakness to sharpen your grasp of the subject and our top tips for revision and sitting the exam will also help to improve your performance on the day.

Remember, practice makes perfect! These past papers will show you what to expect in your exam, help to boost your confidence and feel ready to gain the grade you really want.

Good luck!

Acknowledgements

Every effort has been made to trace the copyright holders and to obtain their permission for the use of copyright material. Leckie & Leckie will gladly receive information enabling them to rectify any error or omission in subsequent editions.

1998 CREDIT

Official SQA Past Papers: Credit Physics 1998

FOR OFFICIAL USE

Presenting Centre No.	Subject No. 3220	Level	Paper No.	Group No.	Marker's No.

C

K & U   PS

Total Marks

3220/102

SCOTTISH CERTIFICATE OF EDUCATION 1998

FRIDAY, 15 MAY
10.45 AM – 12.30 PM

**PHYSICS
STANDARD GRADE
Credit Level**

Fill in these boxes and read what is printed below.

Full name of school or college

Town

First name and initials

Surname

Date of birth
Day Month Year

Candidate number

Number of seat

1. All questions should be answered.

2. The questions may be answered in any order but all answers must be written clearly and legibly in this book.

3. Write your answer where indicated by the question or in the space provided after the question.

4. If you change your mind about your answer you may score it out and rewrite it in the space provided at the end of the answer book.

5. Before leaving the examination room you must give this book to the invigilator. If you do not, you may lose all the marks for this paper.

6. Any necessary data will be found in the **data sheet** on page two.

SCOTTISH QUALIFICATIONS AUTHORITY

DATA SHEET

Speed of light in materials

Material	Speed in m/s
Air	3.0×10^8
Carbon dioxide	3.0×10^8
Diamond	1.2×10^8
Glass	2.0×10^8
Glycerol	2.1×10^8
Water	2.3×10^8

Speed of sound in materials

Material	Speed in m/s
Aluminium	5200
Air	340
Bone	4100
Carbon dioxide	270
Glycerol	1900
Muscle	1600
Steel	5200
Tissue	1500
Water	1500

Gravitational field strengths

	Gravitational field strength on the surface in N/kg
Earth	10
Jupiter	26
Mars	4
Mercury	4
Moon	1.6
Neptune	12
Saturn	11
Sun	270
Venus	9

Specific heat capacity of materials

Material	Specific heat capacity in J/kg °C
Alcohol	2350
Aluminium	902
Copper	386
Diamond	530
Glass	500
Glycerol	2400
Ice	2100
Lead	128
Water	4180

Specific latent heat of fusion of materials

Material	Specific latent heat of fusion in J/kg
Alcohol	0.99×10^5
Aluminium	3.95×10^5
Carbon dioxide	1.80×10^5
Copper	2.05×10^5
Glycerol	1.81×10^5
Lead	0.25×10^5
Water	3.34×10^5

Melting and boiling points of materials

Material	Melting point in °C	Boiling point in °C
Alcohol	−98	65
Aluminium	660	2470
Copper	1077	2567
Glycerol	18	290
Lead	328	1737
Turpentine	−10	156

Specific latent heat of vaporisation of materials

Material	Specific latent heat of vaporisation in J/kg
Alcohol	11.2×10^5
Carbon dioxide	3.77×10^5
Glycerol	8.30×10^5
Turpentine	2.90×10^5
Water	22.6×10^5

SI Prefixes and Multiplication Factors

Prefix	Symbol	Factor	
giga	G	1 000 000 000	$= 10^9$
mega	M	1 000 000	$= 10^6$
kilo	k	1000	$= 10^3$
milli	m	0.001	$= 10^{-3}$
micro	μ	0.000 001	$= 10^{-6}$
nano	n	0.000 000 001	$= 10^{-9}$

Marks

1. Information may be passed between a telephone exchange and a receiver in a number of ways.

    (a) Electrical signals from the telephone exchange are converted to light signals. The light signals are then transmitted through an optical fibre to the receiver.

    Complete the diagram in figure 1 to show the path of a ray of light as it passes along the optical fibre.

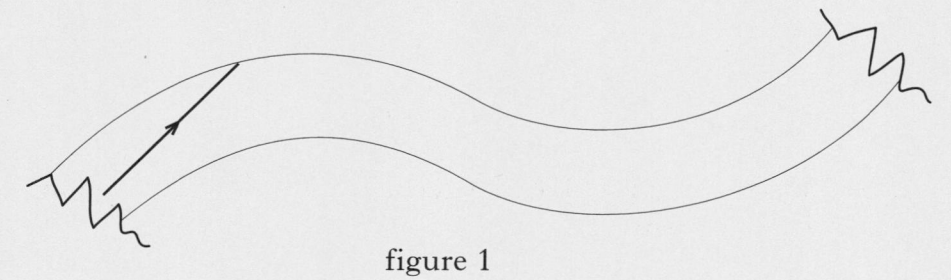

    figure 1 **(1)**

    (b) Electrical signals from the telephone exchange are converted to microwaves. The microwaves are transmitted via a satellite to the receiver as shown in figure 2.

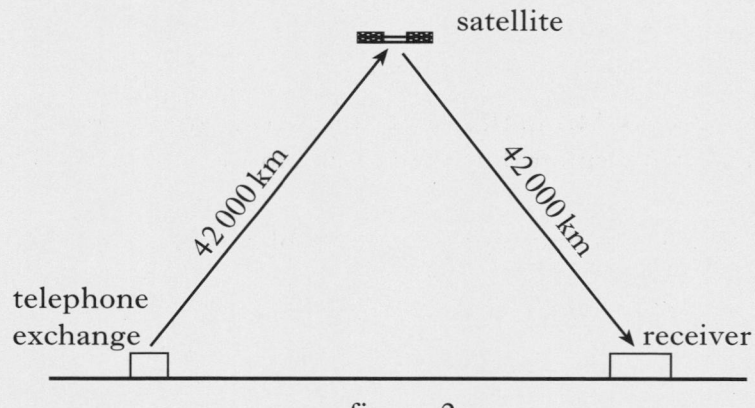

    figure 2

    Calculate the time taken for the microwave signal to travel from the telephone exchange to the receiver.

    Space for working and answer

    (3)

    [Turn over

2. (a) Firefighters use special viewers which detect radiations from the part of the electromagnetic spectrum marked Q in figure 1.

| Gamma rays | X-rays | P | Visible | Q | Micro-waves | TV | Radio |

figure 1

(i) Name radiation Q.

.... **(1)**

(ii) Describe how the viewer is able to detect an unconscious person in a dark, smoke-filled room.

....

....

.... **(1)**

(b) The display screen on the viewer produces a black and white picture.

A pupil suggests that it would be better to produce a colour picture on the screen using a system of phosphor dots which can emit red, green or blue light.

Which dots would glow to produce cyan on the display screen?

.... **(1)**

3. An electric shower unit is supplied with cold water at a temperature of 16 °C as shown below. An electric heater in the unit is used to increase the temperature of the water so that it comes out of the shower at 40 °C. The shower provides 5 kg of hot water every minute.

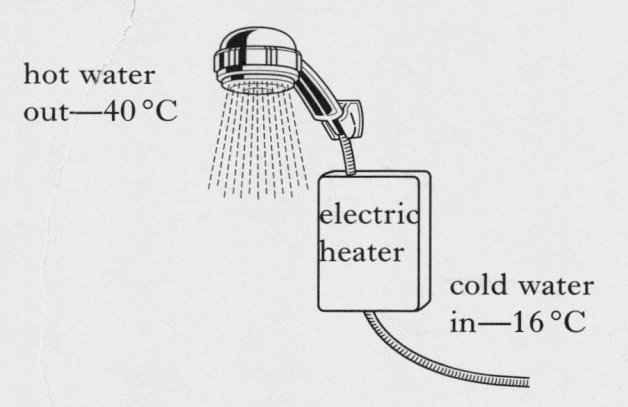

(a) Calculate the heat energy supplied to the water every minute.
   [specific heat capacity of water = 4 180 J/kg °C]

   Space for working and answer (2)

(b) Calculate the power output of the heater **in watts**.

   Space for working and answer (2)

(c) The manufacturer of the shower states that the flow rate may have to be adjusted in winter if a hot water temperature of 40 °C is to be maintained. Explain whether the flow rate would be greater or less than 5 kg per minute.

   ....

   ....

   .... (2)

4. A car starter motor is operated when the driver closes the ignition switch.

Figure 1 shows the system used to operate the starter motor.

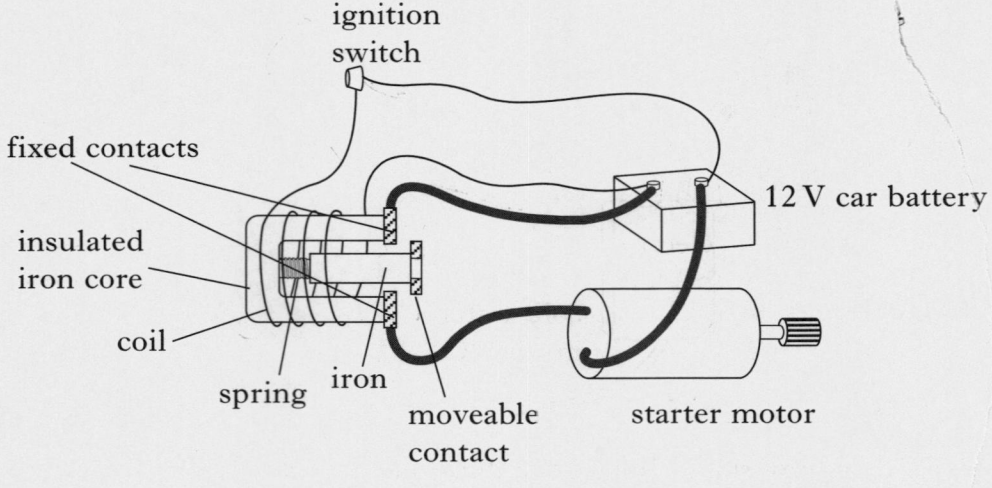

figure 1

(a) Explain why closing the ignition switch makes the starter motor operate.

....

....

....

.... (3)

(b) The voltage across the cable connecting the battery to the starter motor is 0·25 V when the current in the cable is 400 A. The cable has a resistance of 5×10^{-4} ohm per metre.

Calculate the length of this cable.

Space for working and answer

(3)

4. **(continued)**

   (c) A diagram of the starter motor is shown in figure 2.

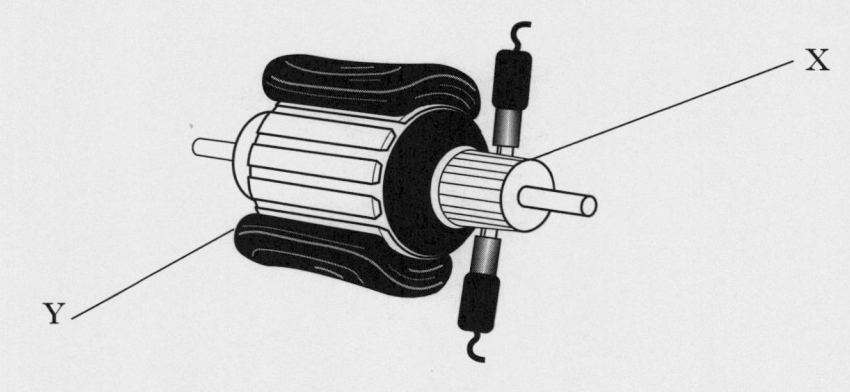

   figure 2

   Name the parts labelled X and Y on the diagram.

   X .... Y .... (1)

   (d) When the starter motor operates, a charge of 360 C is drawn from the battery.

   How long will it take to recharge the battery if a charging current of 5 A is used?

   Space for working and answer

   (2)

   [Turn over

5. An illuminated food cabinet, used in a canteen, has warm and hot areas as shown in figure 1. Separate heating elements provide heat for the warm and hot areas.

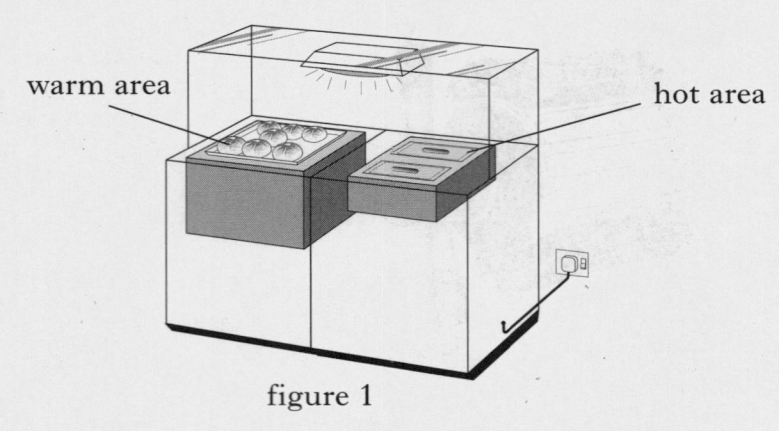

figure 1

The heating elements and lamp are connected to the 230 V mains supply as shown in figure 2. The resistance of each heating element and the lamp is indicated in figure 2.

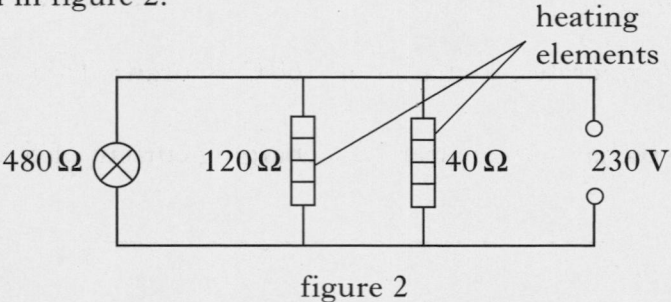

figure 2

(a) Calculate the power of the lamp.

Space for working and answer

(2)

(b) Calculate the combined resistance of the lamp and the heating elements.

Space for working and answer

(2)

5. (continued)

(c) Calculate the current drawn from the supply when the cabinet is operating.

Space for working and answer

(2)

[Turn over

6. A motorist has to wear spectacles to read the number plate on a car which is 20 m away. However, the information on the instrument panel in a car can be read easily by the motorist without wearing spectacles.

(a) Explain whether the spectacle lenses are convex or concave.
(*You may draw diagrams to illustrate your answer if you wish.*)

Space for answer

....

....

....

....

....

(3)

(b) The focal length of one of the spectacle lenses is 67 cm.
Calculate the power of the lens.

Space for working and answer

(2)

7. Read the following passage about eye protection.

Certain groups of people may be exposed to high levels of ultraviolet light. Their eyes must be protected. Spectacle lenses can be treated with special coatings to give protection.

Scientists who regularly use illuminated microscopes must use protective spectacles. These must allow the maximum transmission of visible light but protect against ultraviolet light.

People taking part in winter sports also require spectacles to protect their eyes from ultraviolet light. The spectacles also cut down light received from the sun and reflected from the snow.

The graphs P, Q, R and S below provide information on spectacle lenses with four different coatings.

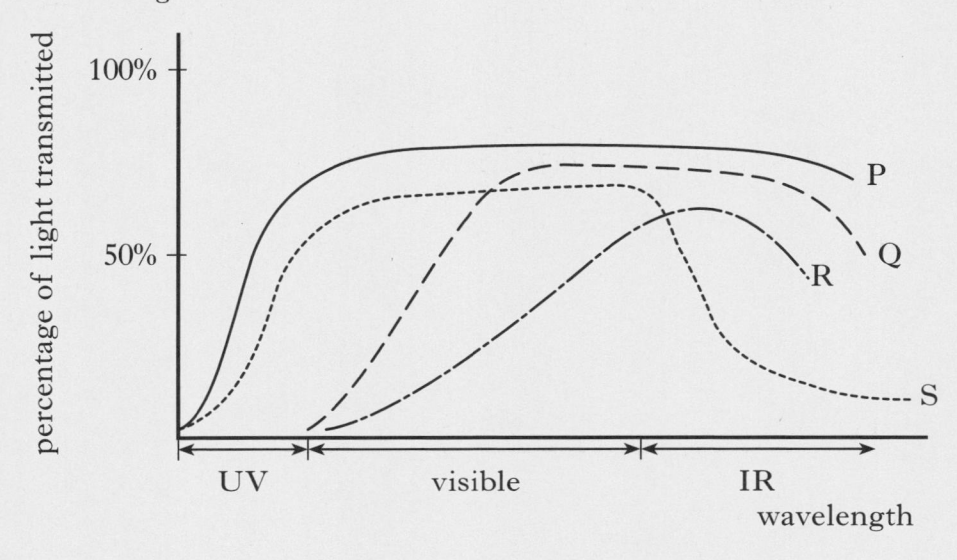

(a) Which spectacle lens should be used by scientists using illuminated microscopes? Give a reason for your answer.

....

....

.... (2)

(b) Which spectacle lens should be used by people taking part in winter sports? Give a reason for your answer.

....

....

.... (2)

[Turn over

8. Doctors use radioactive technetium to investigate different parts of the human body. A solution of technetium is injected into the body and a gamma camera is used to detect the radiation emitted.

(a) The half-life of technetium is 6 hours.
What is meant by the term "half-life"?

....

....

.... (1)

(b) The table below indicates the minimum activity of the technetium solutions which are used to investigate various parts of the body.

Part of body to be investigated	Minimum activity of solution (MBq)
Brain	800
Lungs	80
Liver	200
Thyroid	40

A solution is made up with 800 MBq of technetium at 8 am.

(i) What is the latest possible time that the solution could be used for investigating a patient's liver?

Space for working and answer

(2)

(ii) At 10 pm, which part or parts of the body listed in the table could still be investigated using the solution? Explain your answer.

....

....

.... (3)

8. (continued)

(c) The third column in the table below lists values which give a measure of the biological effect of the radiation on the absorbing tissue.

Part of body to be investigated	Minimum activity of solution (MBq)	.... (................)
Brain	800	0·0170
Lungs	80	0·0003
Liver	200	0·0027
Thyroid	40	0·0020

Complete the table by adding the name and unit of the quantity whose value is listed in the third column. **(2)**

[Turn over

9. A pupil is asked to devise a circuit which will switch on automatically a light emitting diode (LED) when a room becomes dark.

Part of the circuit the pupil sets up is shown in the diagram below.

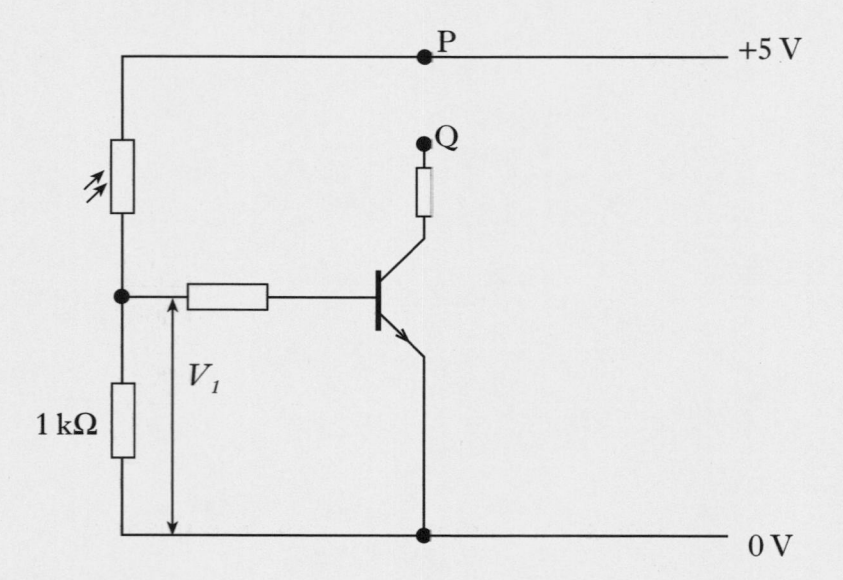

(a) Complete the circuit diagram above to show a LED correctly connected between P and Q. **(1)**

(b) The properties of the light dependent resistor (LDR) in the circuit used by the pupil are shown in the table below.

Lighting conditions	Resistance of LDR
Bright	100 Ω
Dark	10 kΩ

V_1 is the input voltage to the transistor. The transistor switches on fully when V_1 rises above 0·7 V.

(i) Calculate the value of the input voltage V_1 in dark conditions.

(Use an appropriate number of figures in your answer.)

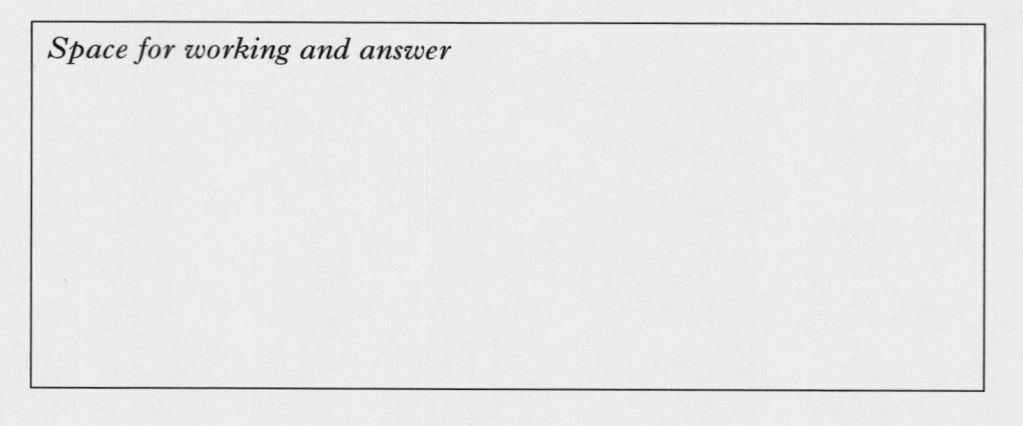

Space for working and answer

(3)

9. *(b)* **(continued)**

(ii) When the room is dark and the LED is correctly connected, it will **not** light. Explain.

....

....

....

.... (2)

(c) Using only the components shown in the circuit diagram, state one change which should be made to the circuit to make it operate properly.

.... (1)

[Turn over

10. A driverless train is operated by sending voltage pulses of different frequency along the railway track to a motor control in the train. The different frequencies of pulse that are used to give different instructions to the motor control of the train are represented by the pulse pattern in the table below.

Instruction to motor control	Pulse pattern
Start train	4 pulses in 1·0 second (voltage 0 to 5 V)
Travel at constant speed	8 pulses in 1·0 second (voltage 0 to 5 V)
Stop train	(no pulses)

(a) State the frequency of the pulses used to start the train.

.... (1)

(b) The pulses are produced by the pulse generator shown in figure 1. The supply voltage is not shown.

figure 1

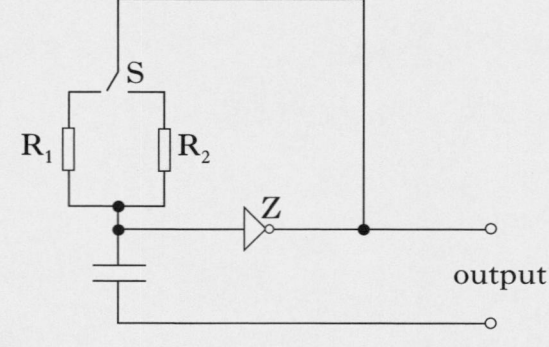

(i) Name component Z.

.... (1)

(ii) Switch S makes a connection with resistor R_1 to start the train and with resistor R_2 to run the train at constant speed.

Which of the resistors has the lower resistance? Give a reason for your answer.

....

....

.... (2)

10. **(continued)**

   (c) The train cannot start until its doors are closed. An electronic circuit is used to give an output which shows whether a door of the train is open or closed.

   The circuit gives an output of +5 V (logic 1) when the door is closed and an output of 0 V (logic 0) when the door is open. Two circuits P and Q are shown in figure 2. Switch S is closed when the train door is closed.

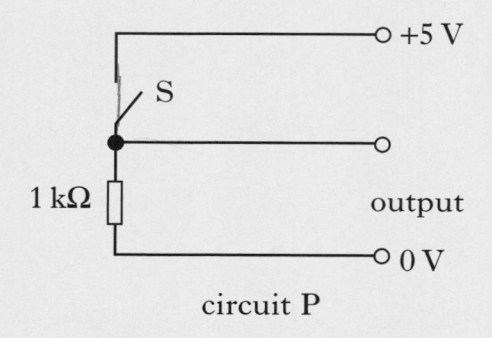

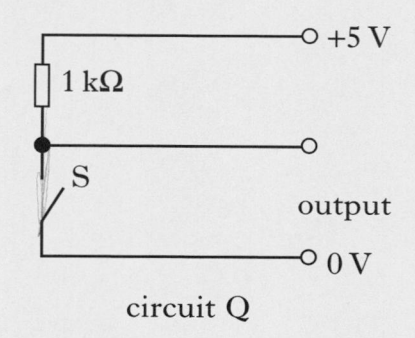

   circuit P   circuit Q

   figure 2

   State which of the circuits P or Q is used and give a reason for your answer.

   ....

   ....

   .... (2)

   [Turn over

11. A roller coaster is designed with a vertical drop as shown below. A vehicle is moved from P to the top of a slope at Q. At the top of the slope the vehicle is released and it falls vertically from R to S.

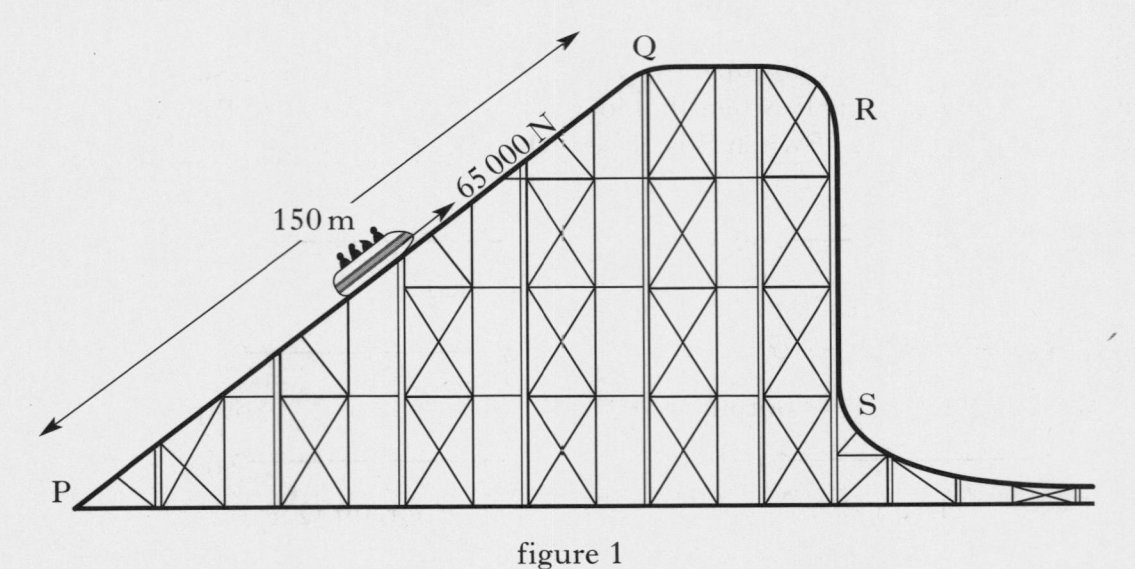

figure 1

(a) A force of 65 000 N is applied over a distance of 150 m to move the vehicle at a constant speed from P to Q.

How much work is done by the force in moving the vehicle?

Space for working and answer

(2)

(b) The vehicle and passengers reach a maximum height of 110 m. The total mass of vehicle and passengers is 8500 kg.

Calculate the potential energy gained by the vehicle and passengers.

Space for working and answer

(2)

11. (continued)

(c) The vehicle is designed to travel at 5 m/s at R and to travel vertically for 4 s to S. A pupil draws a speed–time graph of the motion between R and S as shown in figure 2.

figure 2

Calculate the value the pupil's speed-time graph predicts for the length of the vertical drop from R to S.

Space for working and answer

(2)

(d) In drawing the speed-time graph, the pupil has assumed that the acceleration of the vehicle is 10 m/s^2.

Explain whether the actual value for the vertical drop would be greater or less than the value predicted from the pupil's speed-time graph.

....

....

.... (2)

(e) Describe how the speed of the vehicle at S could be measured.

....

....

....

.... (2)

[Turn over

12. The highway code requires drivers to know about the overall stopping distance for vehicles. The overall stopping distance is made up of:

(1) the **thinking distance**—the distance travelled while the driver "thinks" about braking;

(2) the **braking distance**—the distance travelled while braking.

The following diagram gives information about the overall stopping distance of a car and the time for the car to come to rest under different conditions. Timing starts from the moment the driver recognises there is a need to brake and stops when the car comes to a halt.

	Thinking distance	Braking distance	Overall stopping distance
Car and driver Speed 20 m/s Dry road	14 m	35 m	49 m
Car and driver Speed 20 m/s Wet road	14 m	60 m	74 m
Car and driver plus three passengers Speed 20 m/s Dry road	14 m	47 m	61 m

Time in s   0   0·7   4·2   5·4   6·7

(a) Explain why the thinking distance is the same for the different conditions.

....

.... (2)

(b) Calculate the deceleration of the car on the wet road.

Space for working and answer

(2)

12. (continued)

(c) The total mass of the car and driver is 1500 kg.

Calculate the unbalanced force on the car while braking on the wet road.

Space for working and answer

(2)

(d) Explain why the stopping distance on a dry road increases when the car has passengers.

....

....

.... (2)

[Turn over

13. Electrical power may be provided to remote homes by a combination of wind and solar generators as shown in the diagram below.

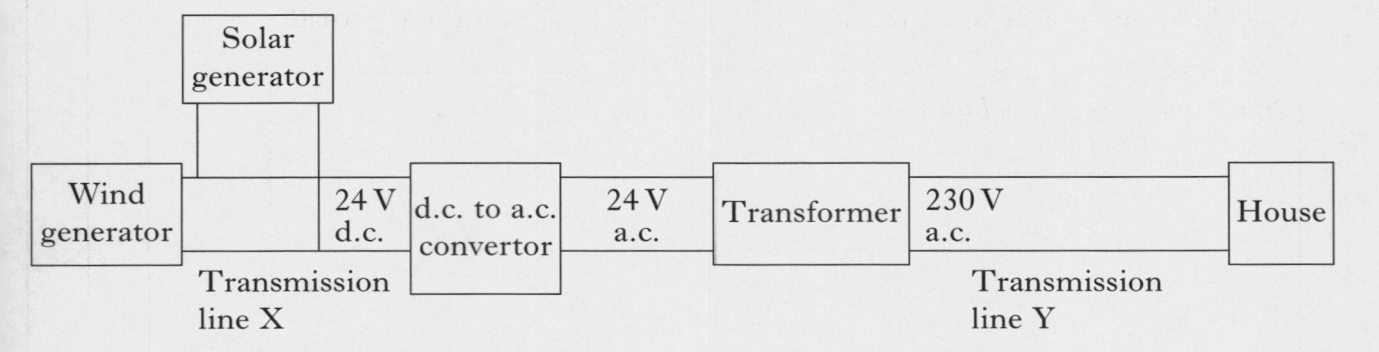

[Diagram: Wind generator → Transmission line X (24 V d.c.) — Solar generator feeds in — d.c. to a.c. convertor → 24 V a.c. → Transformer → 230 V a.c. → Transmission line Y → House]

(a) The following graphs show how the average wind speed and average daily sunlight vary over a year.

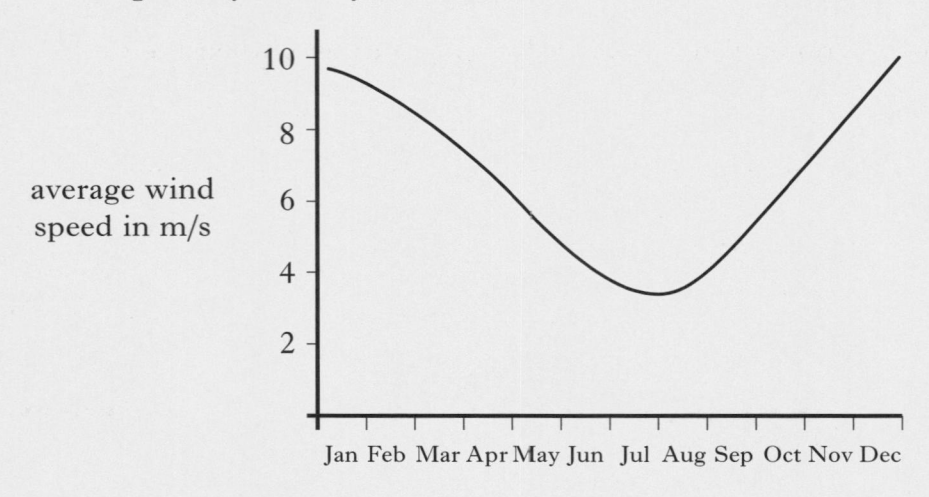

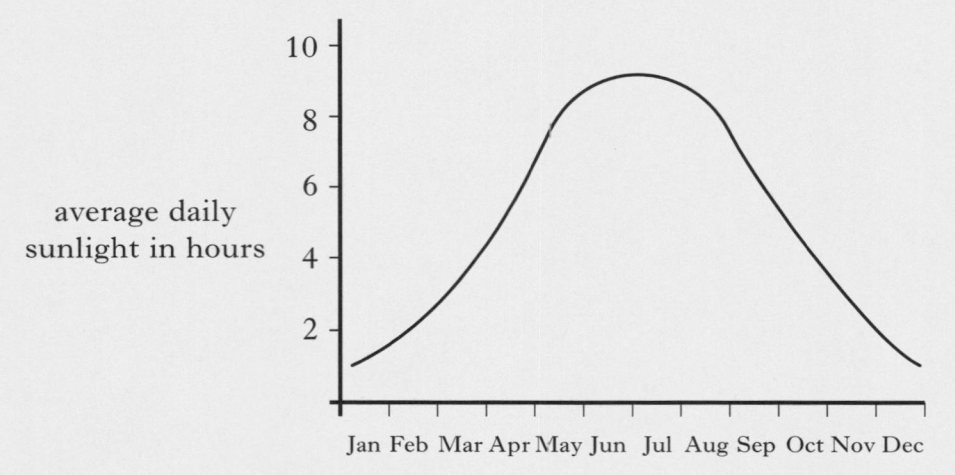

[Graph 1: average wind speed in m/s vs months Jan–Dec; high (~10) in Jan, dips to ~3.5 in Jul/Aug, rises back to ~10 in Dec]

[Graph 2: average daily sunlight in hours vs months Jan–Dec; low (~1) in Jan, peaks ~9 in Jun/Jul, back to ~1 in Dec]

Explain why the combination of wind and solar generators provides an effective system.

....

....

....

.... (2)

13. (continued)

(b) The output voltage from the solar and wind generators is 24 V d.c.

Explain the need for the d.c. to a.c. convertor between the generators and the transformer.

....

.... (1)

(c) The transformer steps up the voltage from 24 V to 230 V. There are 480 turns on the primary coil of the transformer.

Calculate the number of turns on the secondary coil.

Space for working and answer

(2)

(d) The electrical power loss is less in transmission line Y than in transmission line X although the resistance of line Y is greater.

Explain.

....

....

.... (2)

[Turn over

14. (a) Figure 1 shows a space shuttle consisting of an orbiter, called *Discovery*, and booster rockets. At lift off *Discovery* and the booster rockets have a total mass of 2.05×10^6 kg and the thrust of the rocket engines is 2.91×10^7 N. The frictional forces acting on the shuttle at lift off are negligible.

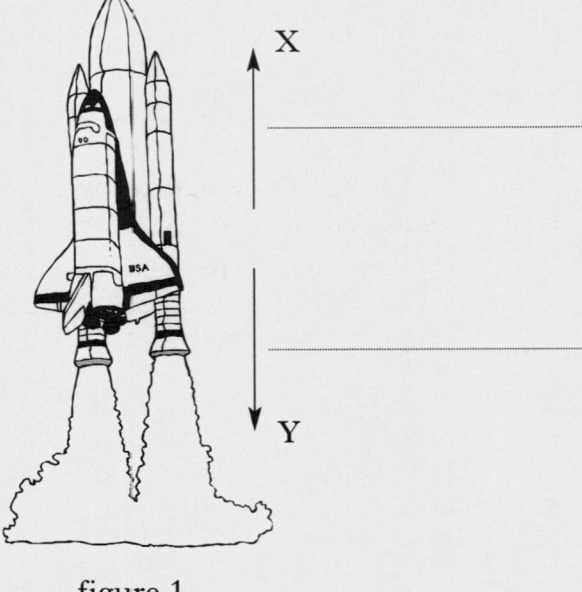

figure 1

At lift off:

(i) label, on figure 1, the two forces X and Y acting on the shuttle in the directions shown; **(1)**

(ii) calculate the weight of the shuttle;

Space for working and answer

(2)

(iii) calculate the acceleration of the shuttle.

Space for working and answer

(3)

14. (continued)

(b) The booster rockets are parachuted to Earth before *Discovery* enters orbit around the Earth. In orbit, *Discovery's* rocket engines are switched off. Figure 2 shows *Discovery* in orbit around the Earth.

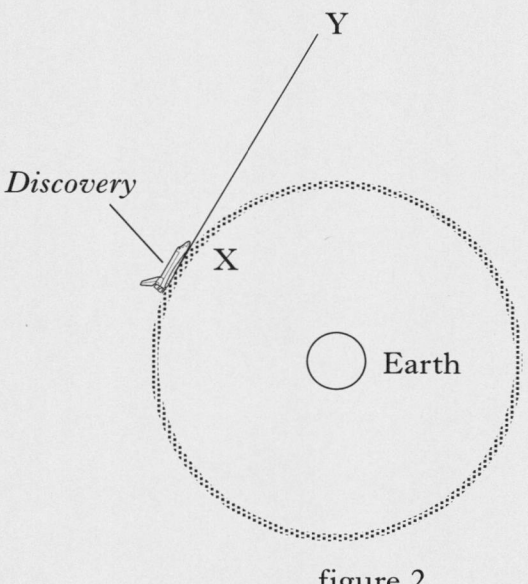

figure 2

Explain why *Discovery* remains in orbit and does not:

(i) move closer to the Earth;

....

....

....

(ii) move off into space along XY.

....

....

....

(2)

[Turn over

15. (a) In 1971, a lunar module carrying two astronauts landed on the Moon's surface. The gravitational field strength on the Moon is different from that on Earth.

(i) What is meant by "gravitational field strength"?

....

.... **(1)**

(ii) The gravitational field strength at the surface of the Moon is 1·6 N/kg.

What is the value of the acceleration due to gravity at the surface of the Moon?

.... **(1)**

(b) One of the astronauts played golf on the moon. The golf ball was struck horizontally from the edge of a steep crater. It landed 2 seconds later, 25 m away as shown in the diagram below.

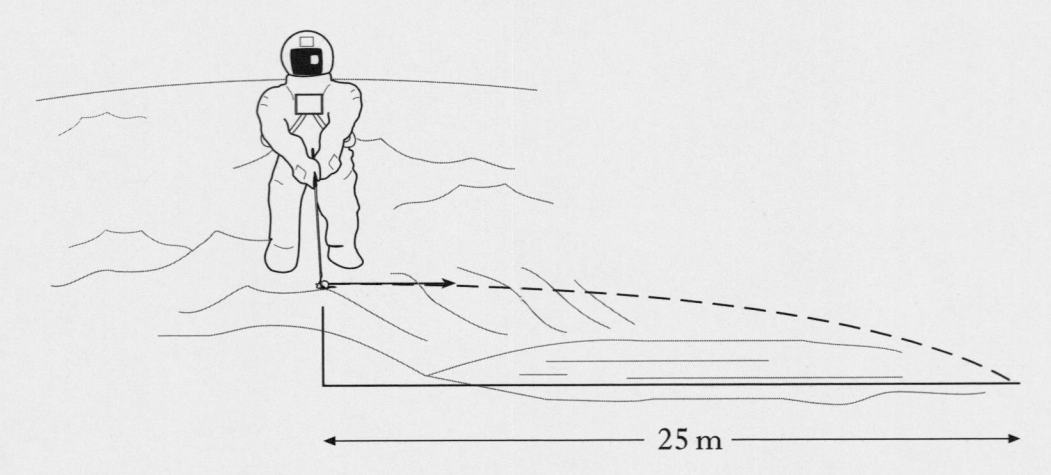

(i) Calculate the horizontal speed of the ball after being struck.

Space for working and answer

(2)

15. (b) (continued)

(ii) Calculate the vertical speed of the ball on landing.

Space for working and answer

(2)

(iii) How would the horizontal distance travelled by a ball projected with the same horizontal speed from the same height on Earth compare with that on the Moon?

Explain your answer.

....

....

....

....

....

(3)

[END OF QUESTION PAPER]

YOU MAY USE THE SPACE ON THIS PAGE TO REWRITE ANY ANSWER YOU HAVE DECIDED TO CHANGE IN THE MAIN PART OF THE ANSWER BOOKLET. TAKE CARE TO WRITE IN CAREFULLY THE APPROPRIATE QUESTION NUMBER.

1999 CREDIT

Official SQA Past Papers: Credit Physics 1999

FOR OFFICIAL USE

Presenting Centre No.	Subject No.	Level	Paper No.	Group No.	Marker's No.
	3220				

C

K & U | PS

Total Marks

3220/102

SCOTTISH CERTIFICATE OF EDUCATION 1999

FRIDAY, 14 MAY 10.50 AM – 12.35 PM

PHYSICS STANDARD GRADE Credit Level

Fill in these boxes and read what is printed below.

Full name of school or college

Town

First name and initials

Surname

Date of birth
Day Month Year

Candidate number

Number of seat

1. All questions should be answered.

2. The questions may be answered in any order but all answers must be written clearly and legibly in this book.

3. Write your answer where indicated by the question or in the space provided after the question.

4. If you change your mind about your answer you may score it out and rewrite it in the space provided at the end of the answer book.

5. Before leaving the examination room you must give this book to the invigilator. If you do not, you may lose all the marks for this paper.

6. Any necessary data will be found in the **data sheet** on page two.

Scottish Qualifications Authority

SAB 3220/102 6/3/3/23120

DATA SHEET

Speed of light in materials

Material	Speed in m/s
Air	3.0×10^8
Carbon dioxide	3.0×10^8
Diamond	1.2×10^8
Glass	2.0×10^8
Glycerol	2.1×10^8
Water	2.3×10^8

Speed of sound in materials

Material	Speed in m/s
Aluminium	5200
Air	340
Bone	4100
Carbon dioxide	270
Glycerol	1900
Muscle	1600
Steel	5200
Tissue	1500
Water	1500

Gravitational field strengths

	Gravitational field strength on the surface in N/kg
Earth	10
Jupiter	26
Mars	4
Mercury	4
Moon	1.6
Neptune	12
Saturn	11
Sun	270
Venus	9

Specific heat capacity of materials

Material	Specific heat capacity in J/kg °C
Alcohol	2350
Aluminium	902
Copper	386
Diamond	530
Glass	500
Glycerol	2400
Ice	2100
Lead	128
Water	4180

Specific latent heat of fusion of materials

Material	Specific latent heat of fusion in J/kg
Alcohol	0.99×10^5
Aluminium	3.95×10^5
Carbon dioxide	1.80×10^5
Copper	2.05×10^5
Glycerol	1.81×10^5
Lead	0.25×10^5
Water	3.34×10^5

Melting and boiling points of materials

Material	Melting point in °C	Boiling point in °C
Alcohol	−98	65
Aluminium	660	2470
Copper	1077	2567
Glycerol	18	290
Lead	328	1737
Turpentine	−10	156

Specific latent heat of vaporisation of materials

Material	Specific latent heat of vaporisation in J/kg
Alcohol	11.2×10^5
Carbon dioxide	3.77×10^5
Glycerol	8.30×10^5
Turpentine	2.90×10^5
Water	22.6×10^5

SI Prefixes and Multiplication Factors

Prefix	Symbol	Factor	
giga	G	1 000 000 000	$= 10^9$
mega	M	1 000 000	$= 10^6$
kilo	k	1000	$= 10^3$
milli	m	0.001	$= 10^{-3}$
micro	μ	0.000 001	$= 10^{-6}$
nano	n	0.000 000 001	$= 10^{-9}$

1. A car passenger receives a call on a mobile telephone while travelling along a road. When the car is at point P in the diagram below, the call is sent from a nearby transmitter T_1.

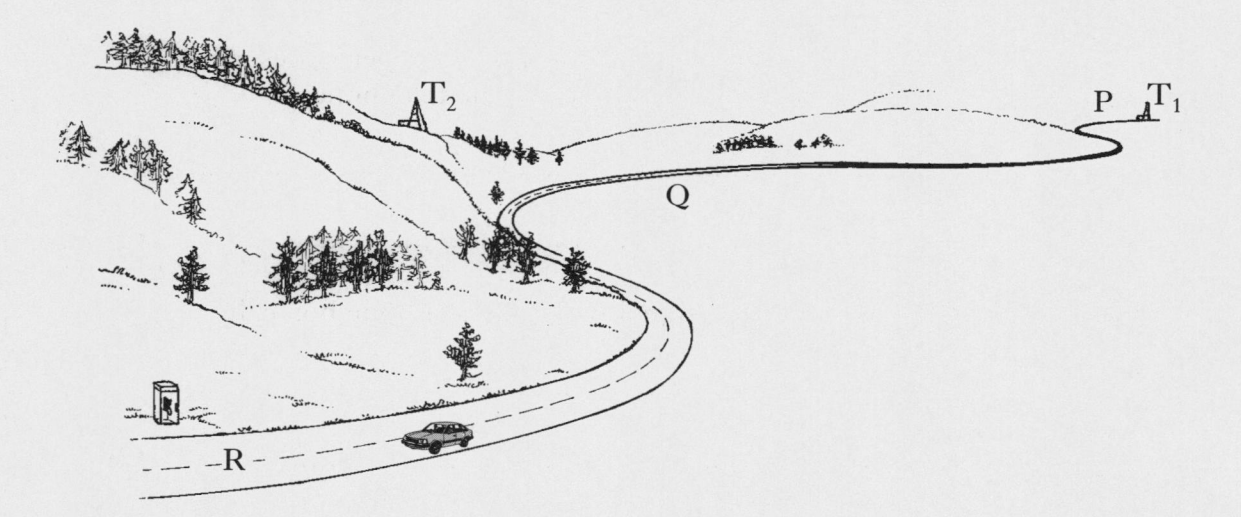

(a) The transmission frequency of T_1 is 900 MHz.

Calculate the wavelength of the radio signal which is used to transmit the call.

Space for working and answer

(2)

(b) At another point Q further along the road, a different transmitter T_2 takes over the transmission of the call.

Using information in the diagram, suggest a reason why a different transmitter is used to send the call.

....

.... (1)

[Turn over

1. (continued)

(c) Further along the road at position R, there is a complete loss of signal when using the mobile telephone. The conversation is continued by making a call from a roadside telephone box.

(i) Assuming the mobile telephone is still working properly, describe what might cause the loss of signal to the mobile telephone.

....

.... **(1)**

(ii) Explain why there is no loss of signal with the telephone box call.

....

.... **(2)**

2. (a) At a science exhibition, a display has two videophones connected together.

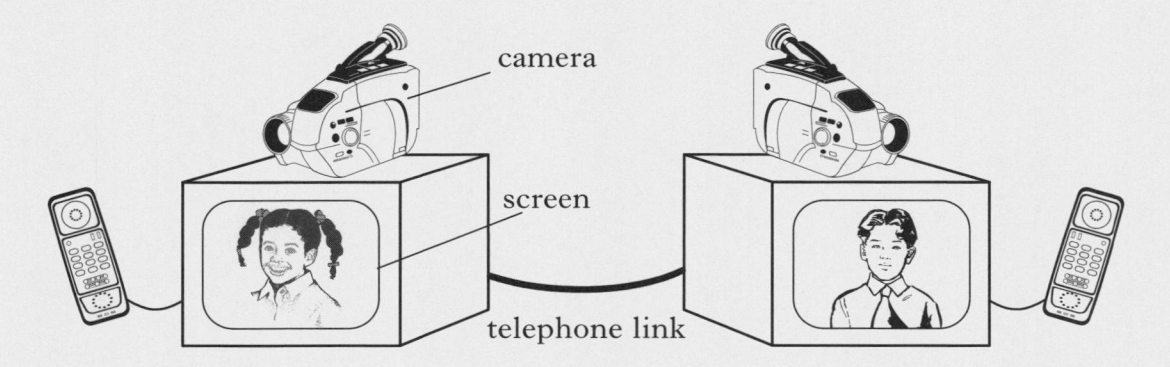

A videophone is a special telephone which can be used to send both video signals (for pictures) and audio signals (for sound) along a telephone link.

(i) A video signal used to test the link produces the black and white pattern shown.

Describe how a black and white pattern is built up on the screen.

....

....

....

.... (2)

(ii) It is only possible to send 3 complete pictures every second along the link to the receiving videophone.

Explain why a person's movement, as seen on the videophone, appears jerky.

....

....

....

.... (2)

2. **(continued)**

   (b) Another display has been set up to show how different colours can be seen on a television screen.

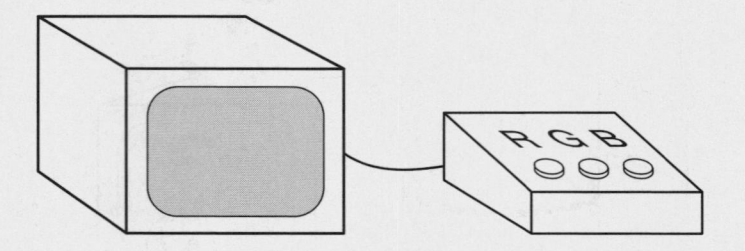

   Switches R, G and B on a panel control each of the electron guns in the television. Each switch turns a gun **off** when it is pressed. The colour controlled by each switch is shown in the table below.

Switch	Colour controlled
R	Red
G	Green
B	Blue

   What colour is the screen when the display is on and

   (i) no switches are pressed;

   ....

   (ii) only switches B and G are pressed;

   ....

   (iii) only switch B is pressed?

   .... (3)

3. The diagram below shows part of a consumer unit in a house. The consumer unit contains fuses for a lighting circuit, a power ring circuit and a water heater circuit, as well as a switch to control all of the circuits. The rating of the fuse used in each circuit is given in the diagram.

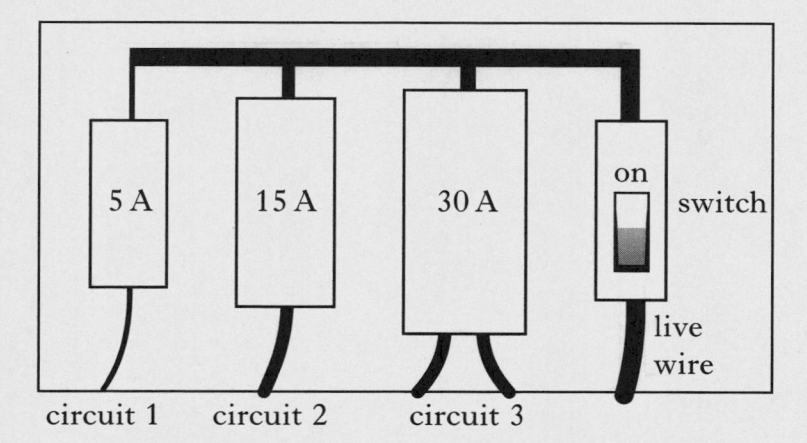

(a) The switch and the fuses are all connected to the live wire of the electricity supply.

Explain why the switch must be connected to the live wire.

....

.... (1)

(b) Explain why identical wire can be used for both circuit 2 and circuit 3 although the fuse used in each circuit has a different rating.

....

.... (2)

(c) What is the purpose of the fuses in a consumer unit?

....

.... (1)

(d) An electrician replaces all the fuses in this consumer unit with circuit breakers.

Give one advantage of a circuit breaker compared to a fuse.

.... (1)

(e) Which circuit is the lighting circuit?

.... (1)

[Turn over

4. A travel iron is fitted with a 3 A fuse. It contains two identical heating elements, each of resistance 92 Ω. The heating elements of the travel iron can be connected for 230 V operation or for 115 V operation as shown in the diagram below.

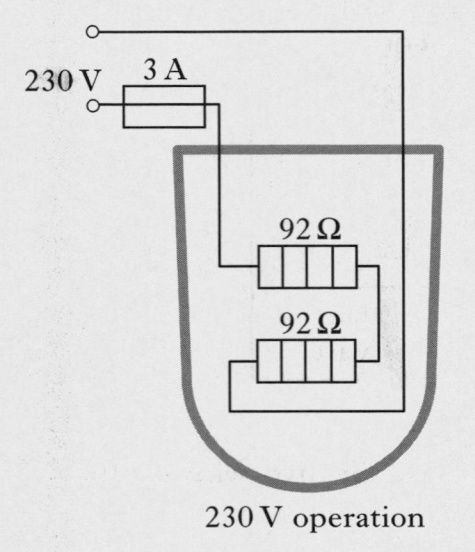

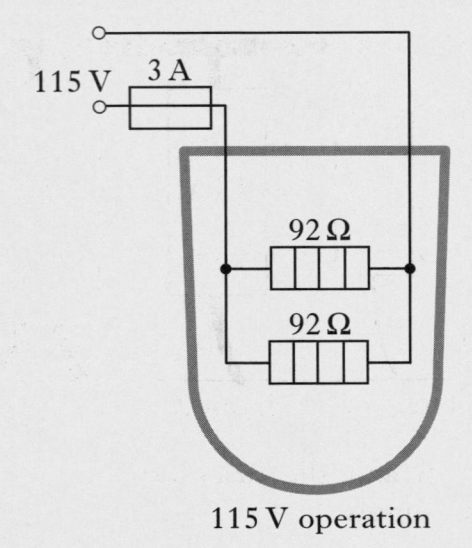

230 V operation: 230 V, 3 A fuse, two 92 Ω elements in series.

115 V operation: 115 V, 3 A fuse, two 92 Ω elements in parallel.

(a) The travel iron is set for 230 V operation and connected to a 230 V supply. Calculate the power developed by the travel iron.

Space for working and answer

(3)

4. **(continued)**

   (b) The travel iron is now set for 115 V operation.

   (i) Show that the combined resistance of the heating elements is 46 Ω.

   Space for working and answer

   (2)

   (ii) Calculate the current in the travel iron when it is connected to a 115 V supply.

   Space for working and answer

   (2)

   (iii) What will happen if the travel iron is connected to a 230 V supply when it is set for 115 V operation?

   Explain your answer.

   ....

   ....

   .... (2)

   [Turn over

5. In the eye, refraction of light takes place at the cornea and the eye lens.

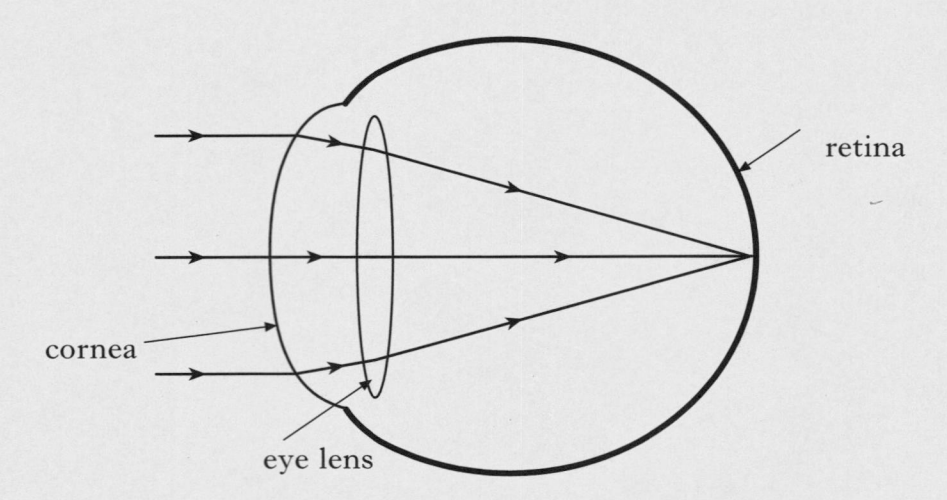

(a) What is meant by refraction of light?

.... (1)

(b) More of the refraction takes place at the cornea as shown above. To show how the eye forms an image, a student uses two identical lenses and a screen to make a model eye. Three parallel rays of light are directed towards the lenses and are focused on the screen as shown.

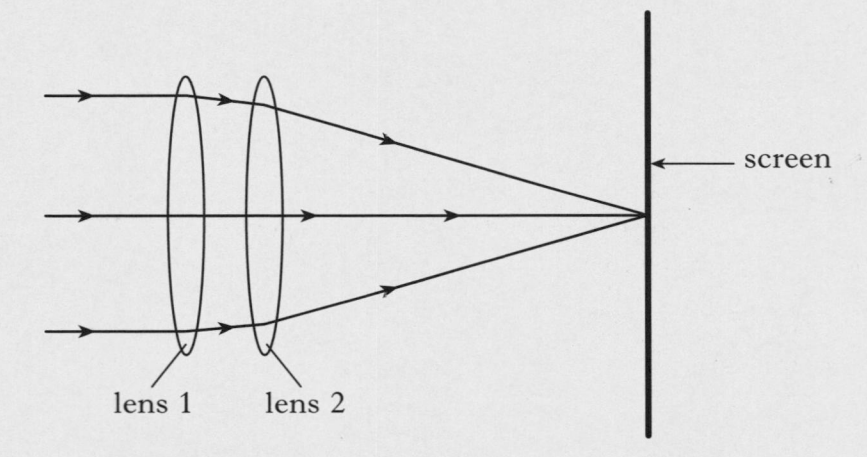

State one change that could be made to the lens system to represent more correctly the eye.

Explain your answer.

....
....
....
.... (2)

5. (continued)

(c) The diagram below represents the eye of a short-sighted person.

  (i) On the diagram, circle the letter where all three rays shown would meet.

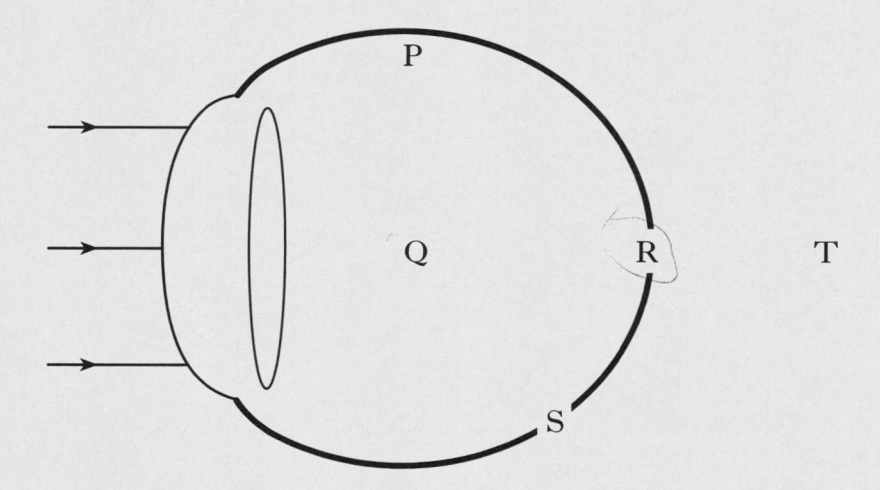

  (1)

  (ii) A lens of power −4·0 D is used to correct for this short sight.

   (A) What is the shape of this lens?

   .... (1)

   (B) Calculate the focal length of the lens.

   Space for working and answer

   (2)

  (iii) Laser surgery can be used to correct short sight by reducing the curvature of the cornea in the eye.

   What effect would the laser surgery have on the focal length of a cornea?

   .... (1)

   [Turn over

6. A radioactive tracer is injected into a patient to investigate the rate at which blood flows in the veins of the legs. The tracer is injected into veins in the feet, and detectors are placed beside both ankles and knees of each leg as shown in the diagram.

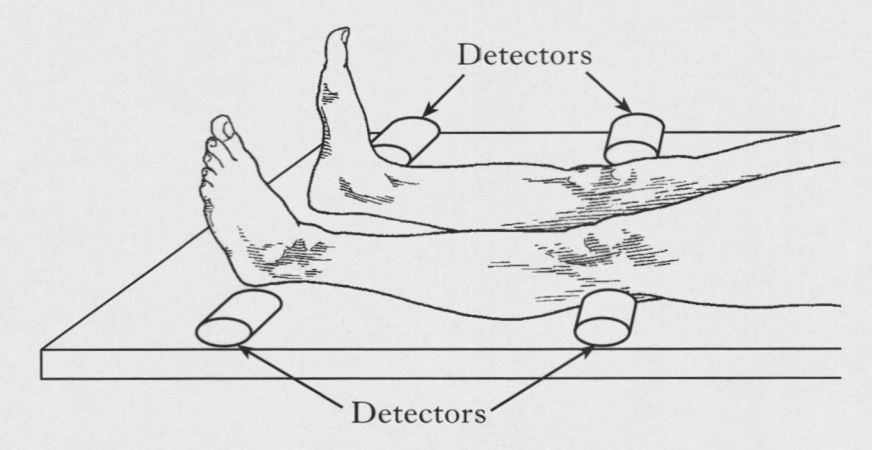

The graphs show how the count rates at the detectors vary for each leg.

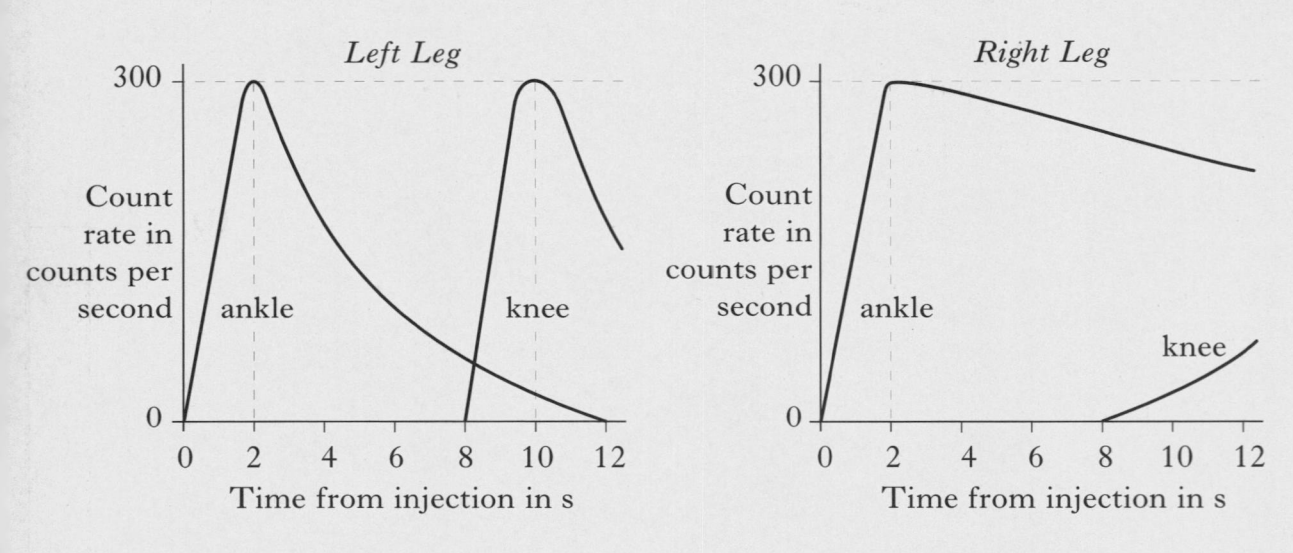

(a) The graph obtained for the left leg indicates that the blood flow in that leg is normal.

How long does it take blood to travel from the ankle to the knee in the left leg?

.... (1)

(b) Explain why the graph obtained for the right leg indicates that there could be a blockage in a vein in the right leg.

....

....

.... (2)

6. (continued)

(c) The hospital keeps three radioactive isotopes for different uses. These are shown in the table below.

Isotope	Half-life	Radiation
Na-24	15·1 hours	gamma
Y-86	14·7 hours	beta
Tc-96	4·3 days	gamma

(i) Which isotope should be selected for the blood flow investigation?

.... (1)

(ii) Why are each of the other two isotopes not suitable?

Isotope: ....

Reason: ....

Isotope: ....

Reason: .... (2)

(d) The patient could also be given an injection of another isotope Au-198 with an activity of 10 kBq. This isotope has a half life of 2·7 days. The patient must be kept under observation until the activity falls to 1·25 kBq.

Calculate how long this will take.

Space for working and answer

(2)

[Turn over

7. A model of a black cat with flashing eyes is made for a Halloween party.

Two LEDs which are used as the eyes are connected to a pulse generator as shown in the diagram below. The output of the pulse generator varies as shown.

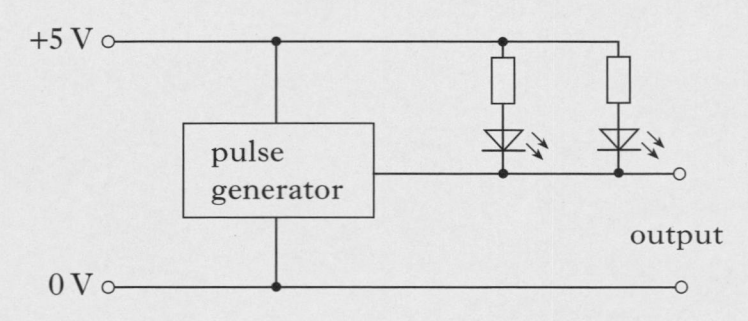

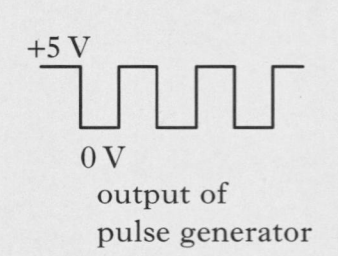

(a) What is the voltage across the output of the pulse generator when the LEDs are lit?

.... (1)

(b) A resistor is connected in series with each LED.

(i) State the purpose of this resistor.

....

.... (1)

(ii) When lit, each LED has a voltage of 2 V across it and a current of 15 mA in it.

Calculate the value of the resistor in series with the LED.

Space for working and answer

(3)

7. (continued)

(c) The diagram below shows a change that was made to the circuit.

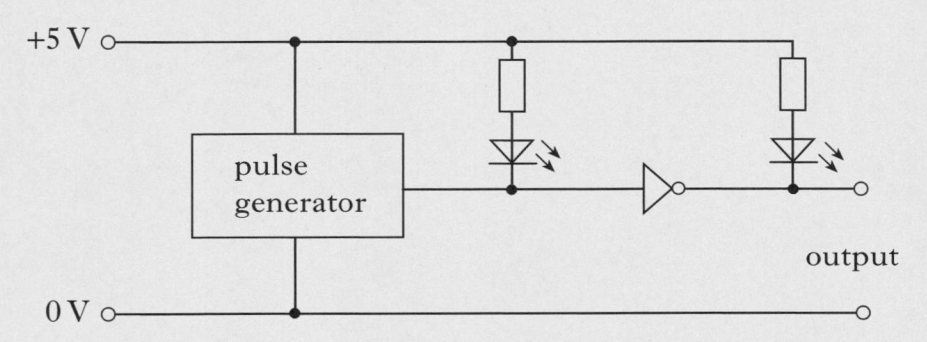

(i) Name the component that has been added to the original circuit.

.... **(1)**

(ii) What effect does this change have on the operation of the LEDs in the circuit?

....

.... **(1)**

(d) The pulse generator circuit is shown in the diagram below. The power supply has not been included in this diagram.

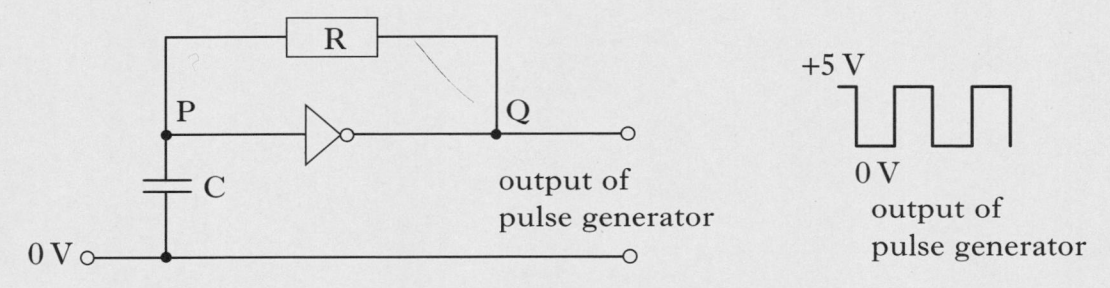

Complete the table to show the voltage at P and at Q when the capacitor in the pulse generator is charged and when it is uncharged.

Capacitor condition	Voltage at P (V)	Voltage at Q (V)
charged		
uncharged		

(2)

[Turn over

8. A jet-engined car of mass 10 000 kg was used to set a land speed record.

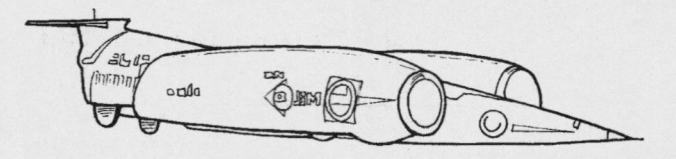

The graph shows the speed of the car during the first part of one test run.

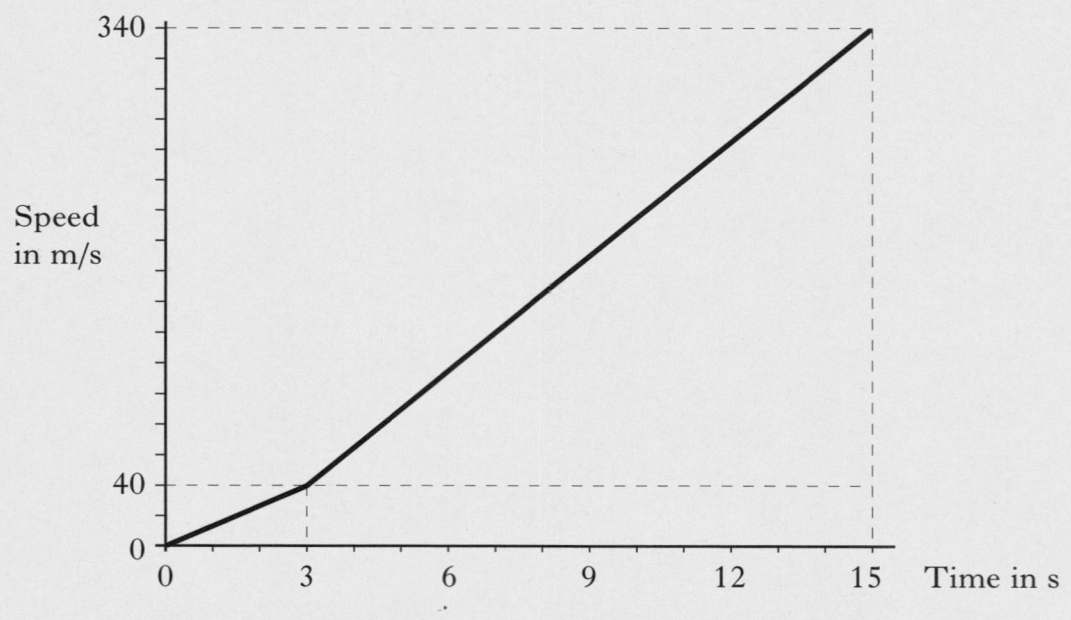

(a) Calculate how far the car travelled during the 15 s shown.

Space for working and answer

(3)

(b) (i) Calculate the maximum acceleration of the car during this part of the test run.

Space for working and answer

(2)

8. (b) (continued)

(ii) Calculate the unbalanced force needed to produce this acceleration.

Space for working and answer

(2)

(iii) During this part of the test run, the force produced by the car's engines was found to be 276 kN.

Calculate the frictional force acting on the car.

Space for working and answer

(2)

(c) At the end of the run, the engines were switched off and parachutes attached to the car were used to slow the car down.

Explain how the parachutes slow the car down.

....

.... (1)

[Turn over

9. A cyclist is riding an off-road course. The combined mass of the cyclist and bike is 80 kg.

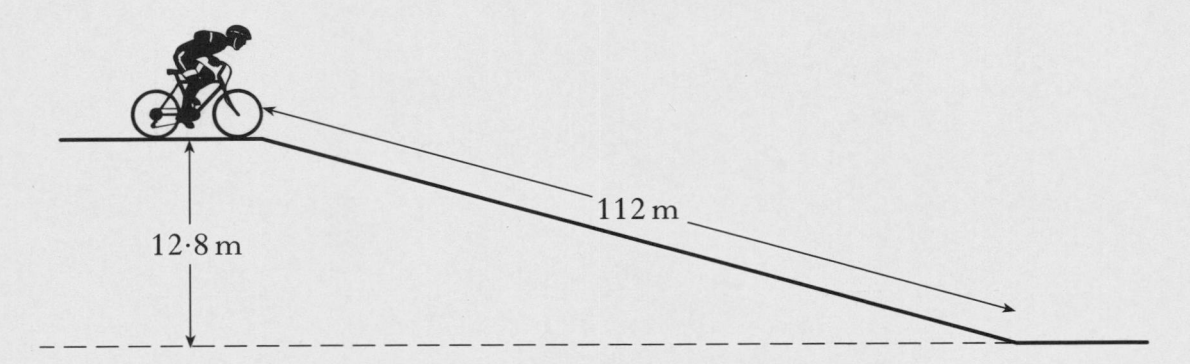

   (a) To get to the start of the course the cyclist has pedalled along a slope of 112 m to the top of a hill of height 12·8 m, as shown in the diagram.

   (i) Calculate how much potential energy has been gained by the cyclist and the bike at the top of the hill.

   Space for working and answer (2)

   (ii) The cyclist then starts from rest and descends the hill without pedalling, keeping the brakes partly on. There is a constant frictional force of 40 N acting up the slope during the descent.

   (A) Calculate the amount of work done against friction during the descent.

   Space for working and answer (2)

9. (a) (ii) (continued)

(B) What is the kinetic energy of the cyclist and bike on reaching the bottom of the hill?

Space for working and answer

(2)

(b) In a later section of the course there is a vertical drop. The cyclist leaves the top of the drop travelling horizontally at 6 m/s and reaches the ground 0·4 s later. Air resistance can be ignored.

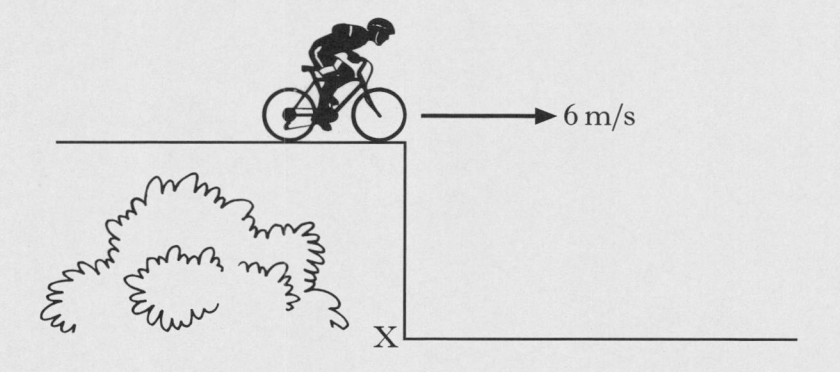

(i) What happens to the cyclist's horizontal speed during the drop?

.... (1)

(ii) What happens to the cyclist's vertical speed during the drop?

.... (1)

(iii) Calculate how far from point X the cyclist lands.

Space for working and answer

(2)

[Turn over

10. A chef uses an electric steamer to cook a fish. The steamer heats water, causing steam to rise through holes in the base of the food compartment.

The steamer is rated at 600 W and contains 0·5 kg of water at a temperature of 20 °C.

(a) Calculate the energy needed to raise the temperature of the water from 20 °C to 100 °C.

Space for working and answer

(3)

(b) The fish has to be steamed for 8 minutes after the water has reached its boiling point of 100 °C.

(i) Calculate the energy supplied to the steamer in the 8 minutes.

Space for working and answer

(2)

10. (b) (continued)

   (ii) Calculate the maximum mass of water that could be converted to steam in this time.

   Space for working and answer

   (3)

   (iii) Energy is needed to cook the fish. This energy comes from the steam when it changes to water.

   Complete the following passage by using the words **heat** and **temperature**.

   When steam changes to water, it loses .... but its .... does not change.

   (1)

   [Turn over

11. A pupil uses a 120 turn coil as the primary of a transformer.

Three other coils, one of 60 turns, one of 120 turns and one of 240 turns are used separately as the secondary of the transformer.

A variable voltage supply and voltmeters are connected as shown in the diagram.

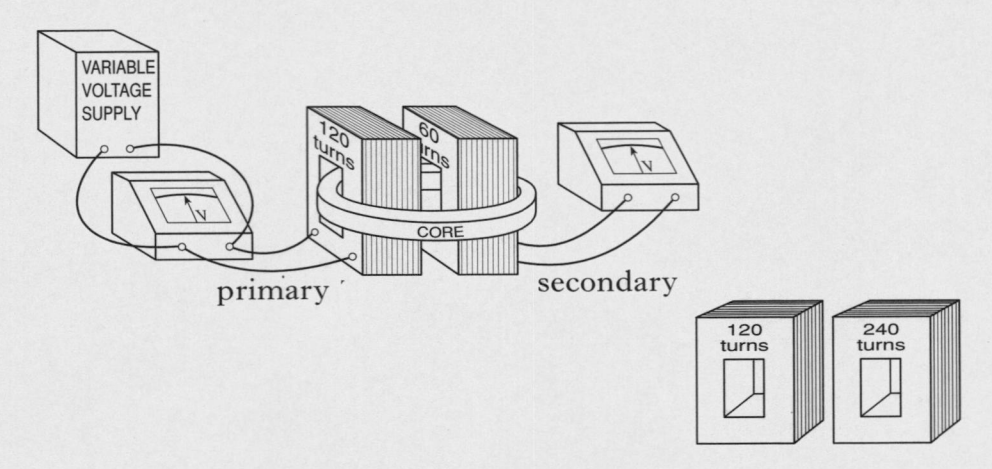

The voltage of the supply is varied.

For each secondary coil in turn, voltmeter readings are taken of the voltage across the primary and the corresponding voltage across the secondary.

The lines X, Y and Z on the graph are obtained by plotting these readings.

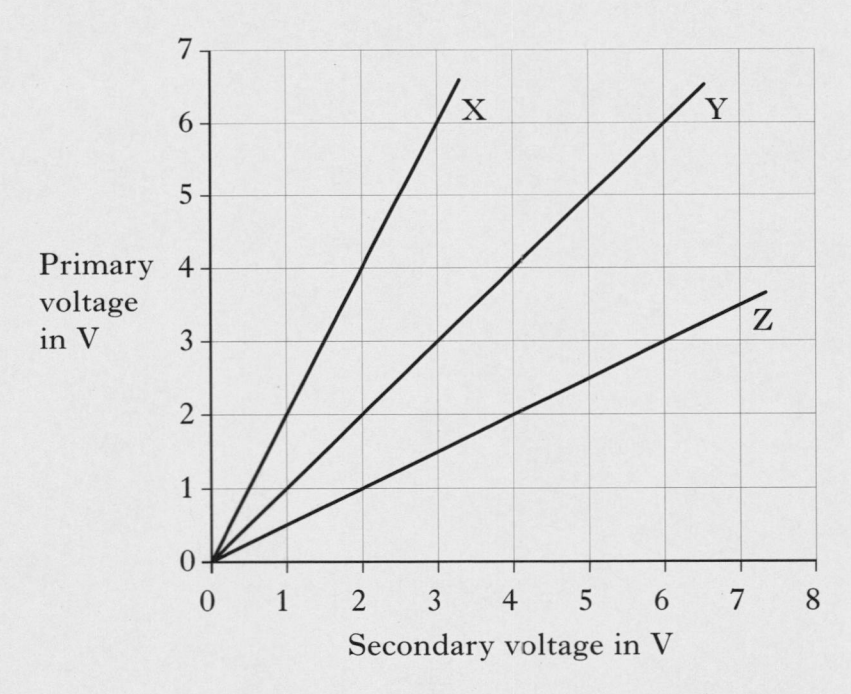

(a) (i) There is a choice of either a.c. or d.c. voltmeters.

Which type should be used in this experiment?

Explain your answer.

....

.... (2)

11. **(a)** **(continued)**

(ii) Complete the table below using information from the graph.

	Primary voltage (V)	Secondary voltage (V)
line X	2	
line Y	2	
line Z	2	

(3)

(iii) Which of the lines X, Y or Z shows the results for a step down transformer?

....

(1)

(iv) Which coil did the pupil use as the secondary coil in the transformer to produce line Z?

Support your answer with a calculation.

Space for working and answer

(2)

[Turn over

11. (continued)

(b) The pupil investigates the efficiency of transformers using a transformer, two joulemeters and a lamp connected to a supply as shown.

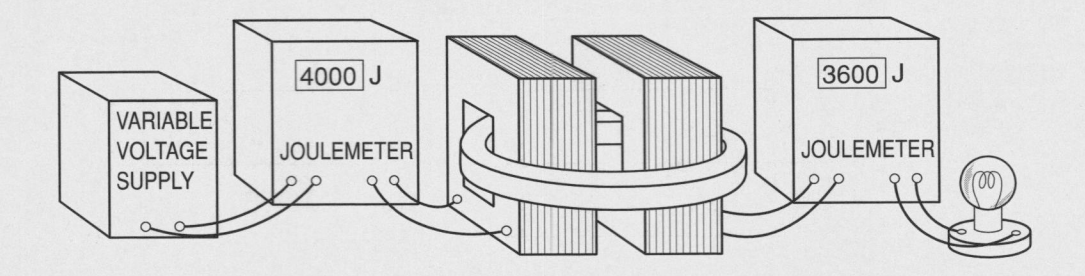

[Diagram: Variable voltage supply → Joulemeter (4000 J) → transformer → Joulemeter (3600 J) → lamp]

Initially, the displays on both joulemeters are set to zero. The supply is switched on and after a certain time the readings shown are obtained.

(i) Calculate the percentage efficiency of this transformer.

Space for working and answer

(2)

(ii) Give a reason why transformers are not 100% efficient.

....

.... (1)

12. Read the following article.

The planet Mars is the fourth planet out from the Sun in our solar system. Mars has very little atmosphere and because of this, its surface is exposed to high levels of ultraviolet radiations.

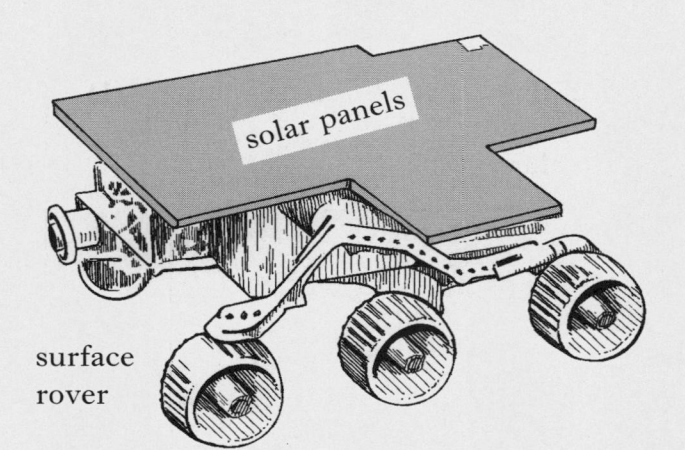

In July 1997 Mars Pathfinder landed on the surface of the planet. Pathfinder consisted of a stationary lander and a mobile surface rover. The lander was in constant communication with Earth and there was a UHF radio communications link between the lander and the surface rover.

The surface rover, of mass 10·5 kg, was powered by solar panels with a total area of 0·2 m² as shown in the diagram. It carried various instruments including an X-ray spectrometer which was used to carry out tests on the surface of the planet.

(a) The passage mentions by name three radiations in the electromagnetic spectrum.

List these radiations in order of **increasing** wavelengths.

Radiation 1	Radiation 2	Radiation 3
Shortest wavelength	⟶	Longest wavelength

(2)

(b) Solar radiation provides 65 W of power to each square metre of the surface of Mars.

(i) Calculate the maximum power output of the solar panels on the surface rover on Mars.

Space for working and answer

(2)

[Turn over for Question 12(b) on *Page twenty-six*

12. *(b)* **(continued)**

(ii) Give one advantage of using solar panels instead of batteries to power the surface rover.

....

.... **(1)**

(c) Calculate the weight of the surface rover on Mars.

Space for working and answer

(2)

[*END OF QUESTION PAPER*]

2000 CREDIT

Official SQA Past Papers: Credit Physics 2000

FOR OFFICIAL USE

C

K & U   PS

Total Marks

3220/402

NATIONAL QUALIFICATIONS 2000

WEDNESDAY, 31 MAY
10.50 AM – 12.35 PM

PHYSICS
STANDARD GRADE
Credit Level

Fill in these boxes and read what is printed below.

Full name of centre

Town

Forename(s)

Surname

Date of birth
Day Month Year

Scottish candidate number

Number of seat

1 All questions should be answered.

2 The questions may be answered in any order but all answers must be written clearly and legibly in this book.

3 Write your answer where indicated by the question or in the space provided after the question.

4 If you change your mind about your answer you may score it out and rewrite it in the space provided at the end of the answer book.

5 Before leaving the examination room you must give this book to the invigilator. If you do not, you may lose all the marks for this paper.

6 Any necessary data will be found in the **data sheet** on page two.

SCOTTISH
QUALIFICATIONS
AUTHORITY

LIB 3220/402 6/3/23120

DATA SHEET

Speed of light in materials

Material	Speed in m/s
Air	3.0×10^8
Carbon dioxide	3.0×10^8
Diamond	1.2×10^8
Glass	2.0×10^8
Glycerol	2.1×10^8
Water	2.3×10^8

Speed of sound in materials

Material	Speed in m/s
Aluminium	5200
Air	340
Bone	4100
Carbon dioxide	270
Glycerol	1900
Muscle	1600
Steel	5200
Tissue	1500
Water	1500

Gravitational field strengths

	Gravitational field strength on the surface in N/kg
Earth	10
Jupiter	26
Mars	4
Mercury	4
Moon	1.6
Neptune	12
Saturn	11
Sun	270
Venus	9

Specific heat capacity of materials

Material	Specific heat capacity in J/kg °C
Alcohol	2350
Aluminium	902
Copper	386
Diamond	530
Glass	500
Glycerol	2400
Ice	2100
Lead	128
Water	4180

Specific latent heat of fusion of materials

Material	Specific latent heat of fusion in J/kg
Alcohol	0.99×10^5
Aluminium	3.95×10^5
Carbon dioxide	1.80×10^5
Copper	2.05×10^5
Glycerol	1.81×10^5
Lead	0.25×10^5
Water	3.34×10^5

Melting and boiling points of materials

Material	Melting point in °C	Boiling point in °C
Alcohol	−98	65
Aluminium	660	2470
Copper	1077	2567
Glycerol	18	290
Lead	328	1737
Turpentine	−10	156

Specific latent heat of vaporisation of materials

Material	Specific latent heat of vaporisation in J/kg
Alcohol	11.2×10^5
Carbon dioxide	3.77×10^5
Glycerol	8.30×10^5
Turpentine	2.90×10^5
Water	22.6×10^5

SI Prefixes and Multiplication Factors

Prefix	Symbol	Factor	
giga	G	1 000 000 000	$= 10^9$
mega	M	1 000 000	$= 10^6$
kilo	k	1000	$= 10^3$
milli	m	0.001	$= 10^{-3}$
micro	μ	0.000 001	$= 10^{-6}$
nano	n	0.000 000 001	$= 10^{-9}$

1. Radio signals from the Olympic Games in Australia are transmitted to Britain. The signals are sent at a frequency of 6 GHz (6×10^9 Hz) to a satellite which is in a geostationary orbit. Using a different frequency, the satellite then retransmits the signals to a ground station in Britain.

    (a) State what is meant by a geostationary orbit.

    ....

    ....

    (b) Calculate the wavelength of the signals which are sent to the satellite.

    Space for working and answer

    (c) One of the layers in the atmosphere is the ionosphere. The radio signals pass through the ionosphere as they travel between Earth and the satellite. Radio waves of frequencies below 30 MHz are reflected by the ionosphere.

    Circle the frequency that is suitable for **retransmitting** the signals from the satellite to the Earth.

        20 MHz   4 GHz   6 GHz

    [Turn over

1. (continued)

(d) At the ground station in Britain, the signals are transmitted as a parallel beam of microwaves to a relay station, using curved reflectors.

Complete the diagram below to show the effect of the curved reflector at the relay station.

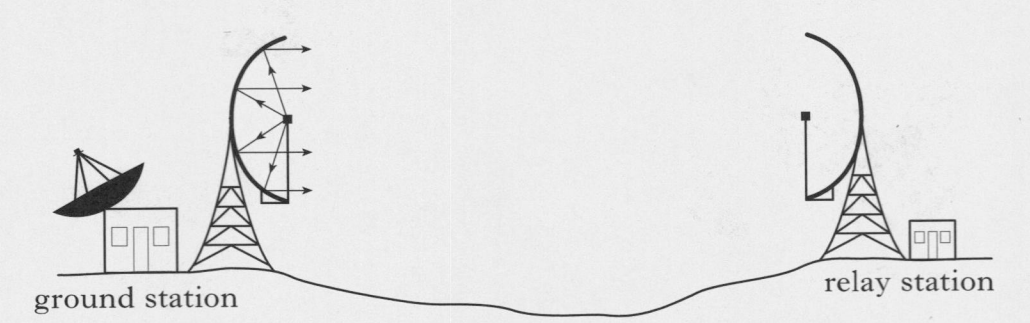

ground station   relay station

2. At a local swimming gala, the swimmers start when they hear the sound of the starting horn. This horn also sends an electronic signal to start timing the race.

At the start of the race, the swimmer in lane 1 is a distance of 2 m from the horn and the swimmer in lane 8 is a distance of 19 m from the horn.

(a) The swimmer in lane 1 hears the sound of the horn first. Calculate how much later the swimmer in lane 8 hears this sound.

Space for working and answer

2. (continued)

(b) As each swimmer finishes the race, an electronic touch sensor detects the swimmer's arrival at the finishing point. After the race, the scoreboard gives the following information.

Place	Lane	Time (s)
1st	1	20·52
2nd	8	20·55
3rd	5	21·91

(i) Using your answer to part (a), or otherwise, explain why the swimmer in lane 8 should have been awarded first place.

....

....

.... **2**

(ii) Suggest an improvement to the starting, or timing, system that would reduce the unfairness of the timing.

.... **1**

[Turn over

3. A floodlight is fitted with a 230 V mains filament lamp. The filament takes 0·5 s to reach its operating temperature.

The graph shows how the resistance of the filament varies after being switched on.

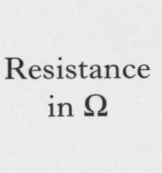

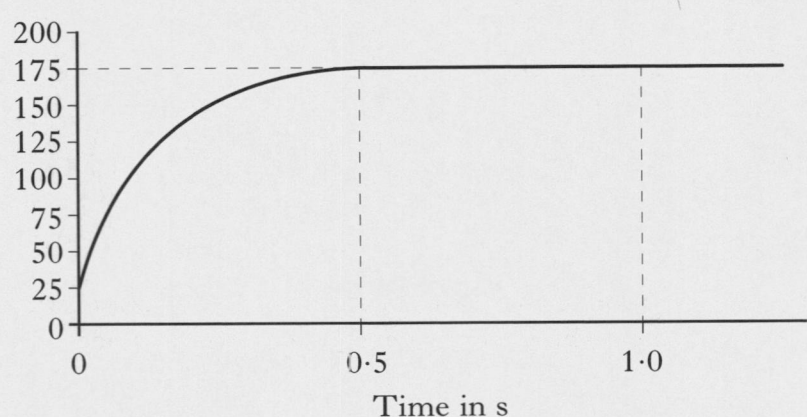

(a) (i) What is the value of the resistance of the lamp when it is operating normally?

....

(ii) Calculate the current in the lamp when it is operating normally.

Space for working and answer

(iii) The floodlight could have been fitted with a lamp with a power rating of 150 W or 300 W or 500 W.

Show by calculation which lamp **is** fitted in the floodlight.

Space for working and answer

3. (continued)

(b) The lamp filament is most likely to "blow" or fail during the first 0·5 s after switch-on.

Using information from the graph, explain why this happens.

....

....

....

....

2

[Turn over

4. A lawnmower has a label which gives the following information.

> Happycutter Manufacturing Co
>
> Model HM96–150 ▣
>
> 230 V a.c. 50 Hz 1500 W
>
> Class II   BEAB approved

(a) (i) State why this lawnmower has only two wires in the flex.

....

....

(ii) State the colours of the insulation on the two wires in the flex.

....

....

(iii) State the value of the fuse that should be fitted in the plug of this lawnmower.

....

(b) Care must be taken to make sure that the lawnmower does not cut its own flex. When this happens, there is a current path from the damaged flex, through the metal handle and the person using the lawnmower, to earth.

A dummy is used to investigate the safety of this lawnmower. In one test, the resistance of the current path through the dummy is 5000 Ω. This is approximately the same resistance as the current path when the lawnmower is used by a person.

4. (*b*) (**continued**)

(i) Show by calculation that the current which passes through the dummy is 46 mA.

Space for working and answer

2

(ii) Explain why, in a situation like this, the fuse in the plug **would not** protect a person using the lawnmower.

....

....

....

2

(iii) What is the purpose of the fuse in the plug?

....

....

1

(iv) Water is now sprayed on the dummy and the investigation repeated. State and explain the effect that this has on the current through the dummy.

....

....

....

2

[*Turn over*

5. Iodine-131 is a radioactive substance which emits beta particles and gamma radiation. A small quantity of iodine-131 is injected into a patient to investigate the thyroid gland. The radiation emitted is detected using a gamma camera.

(a) (i) Why are the beta particles less likely to reach the camera than the gamma radiation?

....

.... 1

(ii) What effect does radiation have on living cells?

....

.... 1

(b) Two safety precautions necessary when using radioactive sources are:
- wear a film badge attached to clothing
- keep as large a distance as possible away from the source.

(i) (A) What happens to photographic film when it is exposed to a radioactive source?

....

.... 1

(B) Describe how information obtained from a film badge is used to indicate the dose of radiation that has been received.

....

....

.... 1

5. (b) (continued)

   (ii) As well as these precautions, a technician wears an additional film badge on a finger when handling a bottle of iodine-131 solution.

   What is the reason for this **additional** film badge?

   ....

   2

   (iii) State one **other** safety precaution necessary when dealing with radioactive substances.

   1

   [Turn over

6. A health physicist is developing a system for measuring temperatures inside the body. A thermocouple is inserted through a tube beside the optical fibres of an endoscope. The endoscope allows the doctor to see where the thermocouple is being positioned. The endoscope consists of two fibre bundles and a "cold light" source.

(a) (i) Explain the purpose of each of the two bundles of fibres in the endoscope.

Fibre bundle P

....

....

Fibre bundle Q

....

....

(ii) What is meant by a "cold light" source?

....

....

(iii) Explain whether a filament lamp or a discharge lamp would be more suitable for the light source of the endoscope.

....

....

....

6. (continued)

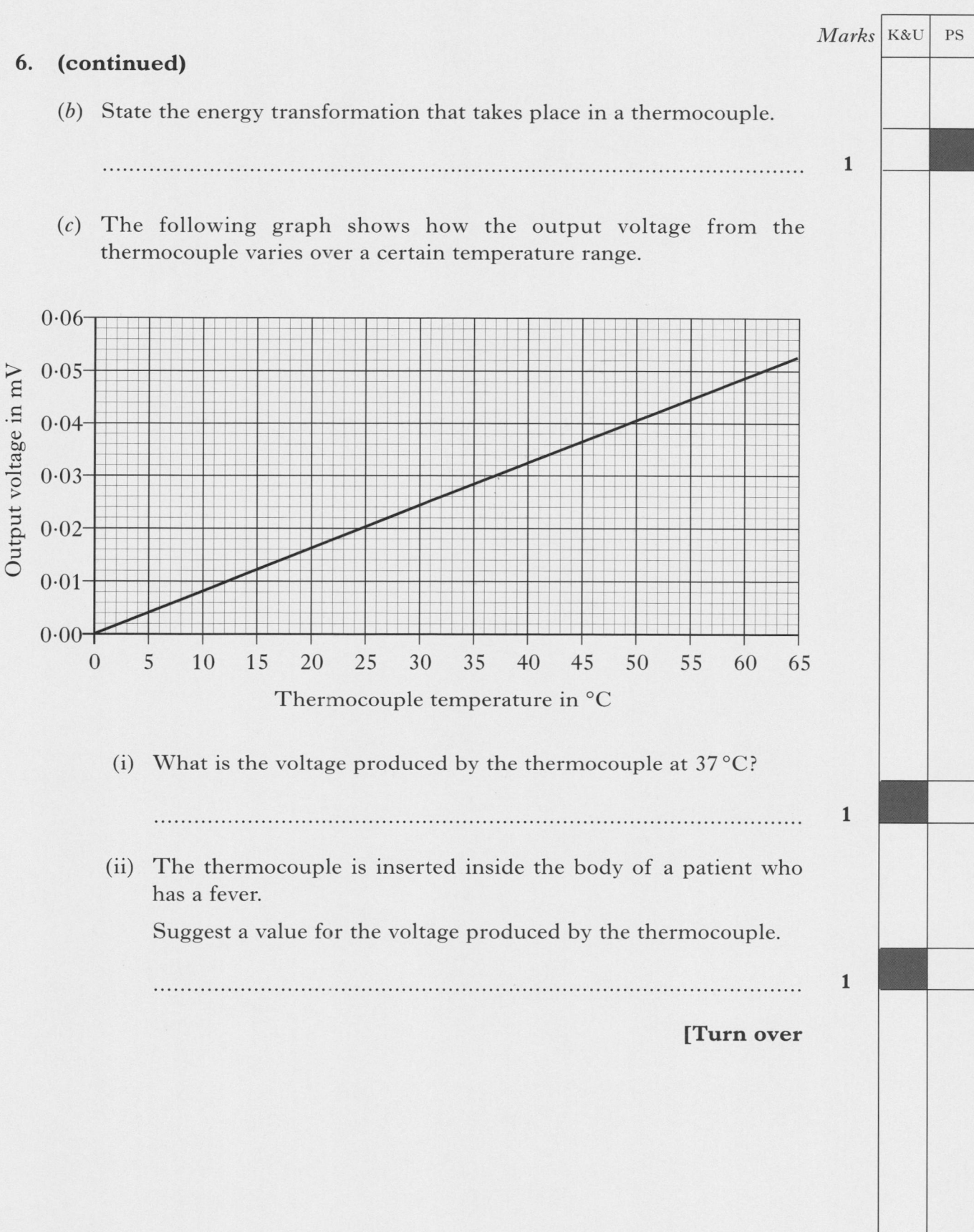

(b) State the energy transformation that takes place in a thermocouple.

....

(c) The following graph shows how the output voltage from the thermocouple varies over a certain temperature range.

(i) What is the voltage produced by the thermocouple at 37 °C?

....

(ii) The thermocouple is inserted inside the body of a patient who has a fever.

Suggest a value for the voltage produced by the thermocouple.

....

[Turn over

7. The electronic system shown is used as a light meter. A voltage is generated when light falls on the solar cell. This voltage is amplified and the output voltage is displayed on the voltmeter.

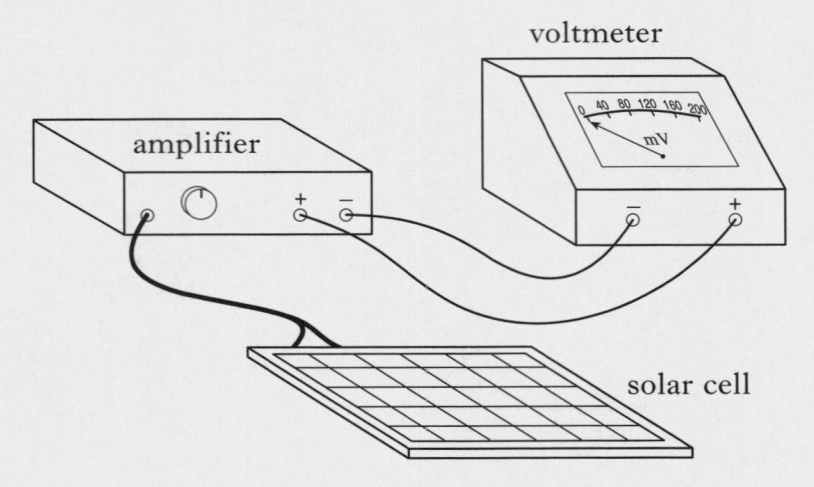

(a) Enter the names of each of the three parts of this electronic system in the block diagram below.

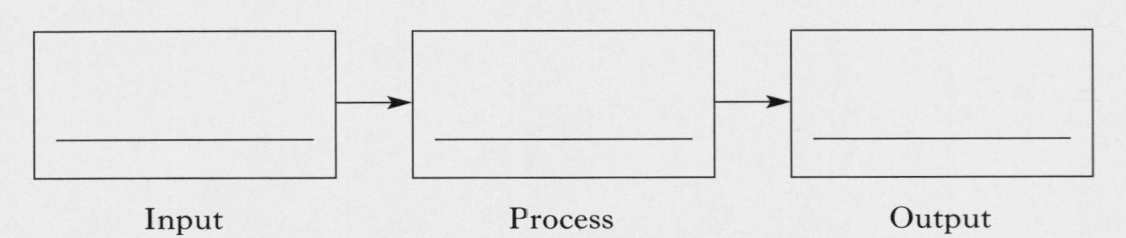

Input	Process	Output

(b) The table shows the voltage generated by the solar cell, and the output voltage of the amplifier for various values of light level. (Light level is measured in lux.)

Light level (lux)	350	400	450	500	550
Voltage generated by solar cell (mV)	0·1	0·2	0·3	0·4	0·5
Output voltage of amplifier (mV)	40	80	120	160	200

(i) Calculate the voltage gain of the amplifier.

Space for working and answer

7. **(b)** **(continued)**

(ii) The solar cell is connected to the amplifier as shown.

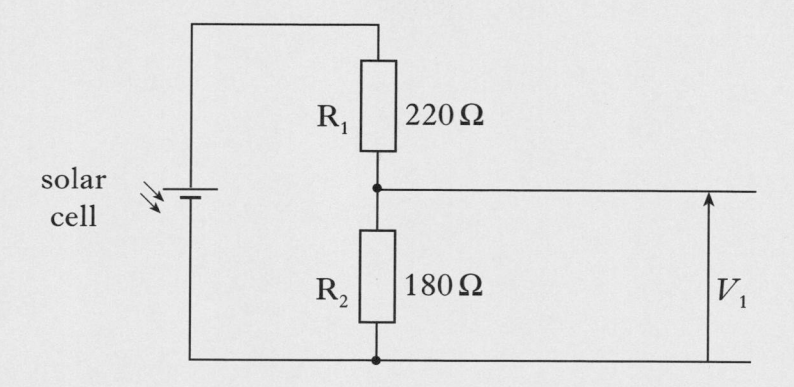

[Circuit diagram: solar cell connected to $R_1 = 220\,\Omega$ and $R_2 = 180\,\Omega$ in series, with V_1 measured across R_2.]

Calculate the voltage V_1 when the solar cell is in a light level of 500 lux.

Space for working and answer

8. A factory wraps cans in packs of six. The cans travel in a single line along a conveyor belt to a wrapping machine which seals them in plastic.

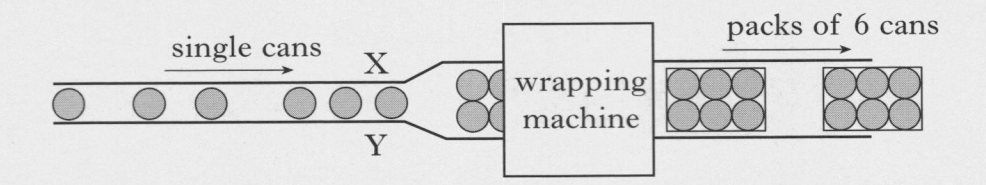

A light beam is set up across X–Y to send a signal to a counter. This signal operates the wrapping machine after six cans are detected.

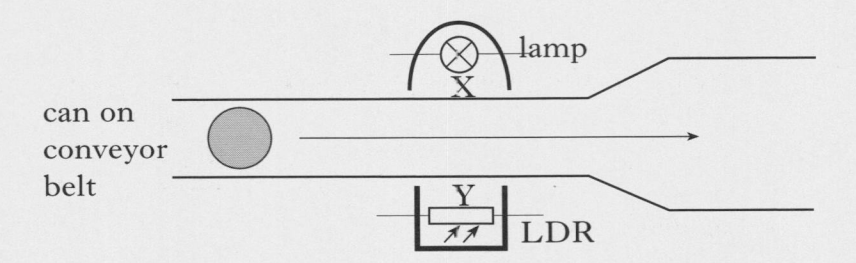

(a) The circuit shown produces the input signal for the counter.

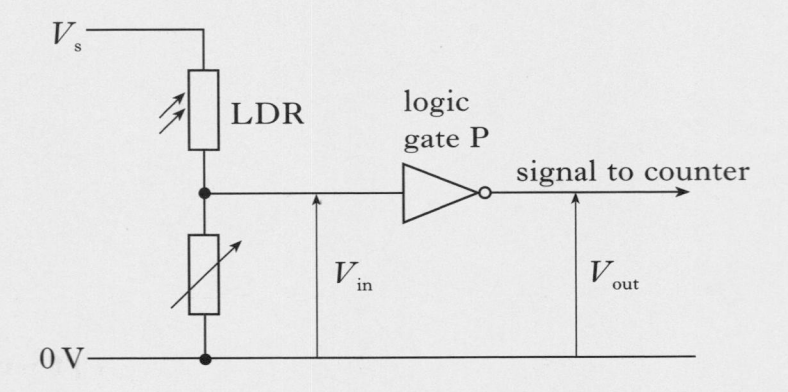

(i) What type of logic gate is P?

.... 1

8. **(a)** **(continued)**

(ii) Complete the following table, writing either **high** or **lo[w]** each entry, to show what happens as cans pass through the beam.

	No can in light beam	Can in light beam
Light level at LDR		
Resistance of LDR		
V_{in}		
V_{out}		

(b) The output of gate P goes to the counter. A 7-segment display shows the number of cans at the wrapping machine. Part of this circuit is shown below.

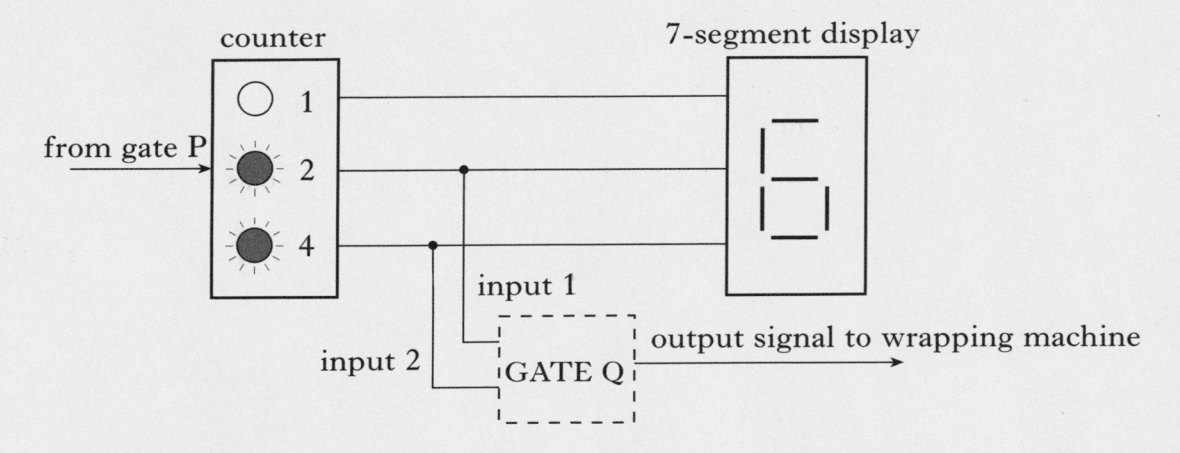

(i) Complete each sentence below by choosing a word from the following list.

analogue   **binary**   **decimal**

The output of the counter circuit is ....

The output of the 7-segment display is ....

[Turn over

(continued)

(ii) Gate Q sends a signal to the wrapping machine when six cans have been detected.

(A) What type of logic gate is Q?

....

(B) Complete the truth table for gate Q.

Input 1	Input 2	Output
0	0	
0	1	
1	0	
1	1	

(iii) There is a short delay to allow six cans to enter the wrapping machine before they are wrapped.

Name a suitable input device that could provide this delay.

....

9. On one road the speed limit is 90 km/h.

(a) Show by calculation that this speed limit is 25 m/s.

Space for working and answer

(b) A speed camera is used to detect motorists breaking the speed limit on this road. A section of the road in view of the camera is marked out with white lines spaced 2 m apart.

speed camera

white lines on road

→ 2 m ←

The camera unit is fitted with a radar speed sensor. When a passing vehicle breaks the speed limit, the camera takes a pair of photographs 0·4 s apart.

When the speed camera film is later analysed, the following pair of photographs is obtained.

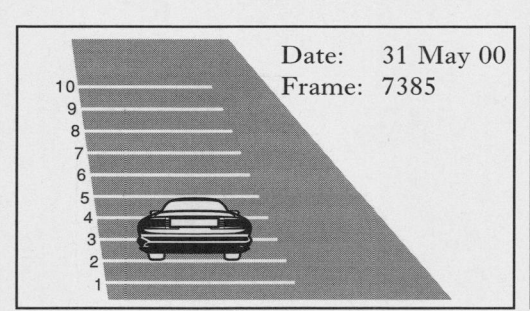

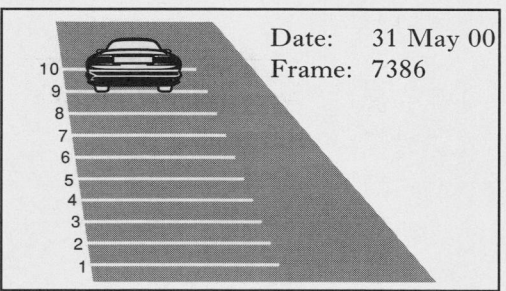

Date: 31 May 00 Frame: 7385

Date: 31 May 00 Frame: 7386

Calculate how much **faster** than the speed limit of 25 m/s this car was travelling.

Space for working and answer

9. (continued)

(c) Further along the road, a sports car travelling at a constant speed of 40 m/s passes a police car which is parked in a lay-by. The police car follows the sports car.

The speed-time graph shows the motion of both cars from the time the sports car passes the parked police car.

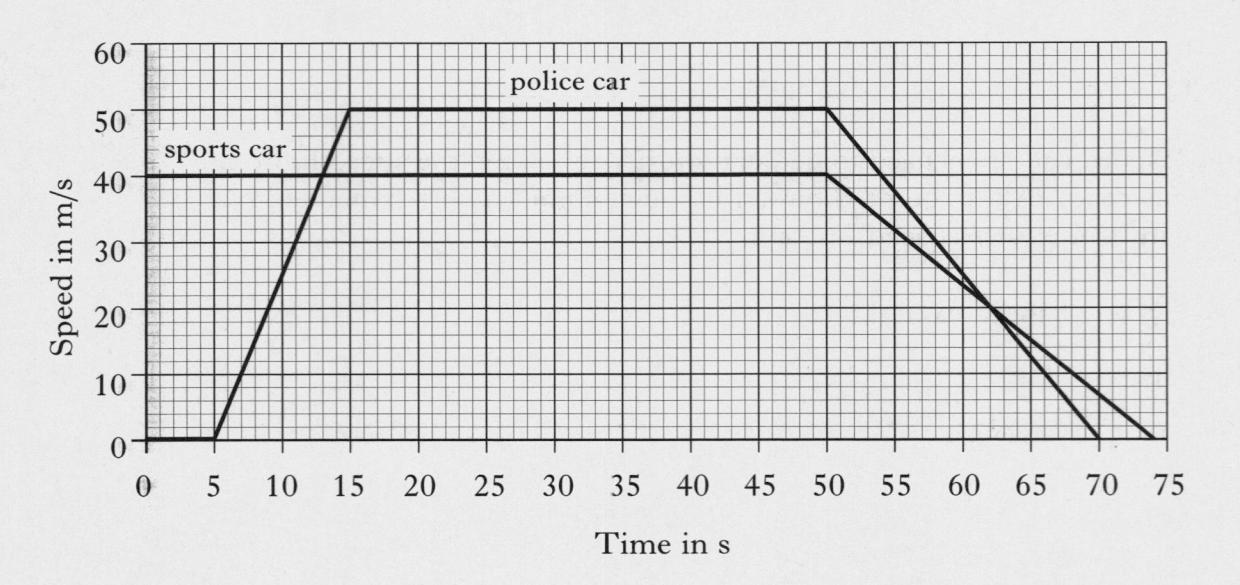

(i) How long does it take for the police car to start to move?

....

(ii) Calculate the acceleration of the police car when it sets off.

Space for working and answer

9. (c) (continued)

(iii) Fifty seconds (50 s) after being passed by the sports car, the police car has travelled 2000 m.

Show by calculation that the cars are side by side at this time.

Space for working and answer

2

(iv) By calculating the distance travelled by each car while decelerating, show which car stops in front **and** the distance between them when both cars are stopped.

Space for working and answer

3

[Turn over

10. An electric storage heater contains a heating element, thermal blocks and insulation as shown in the diagram.

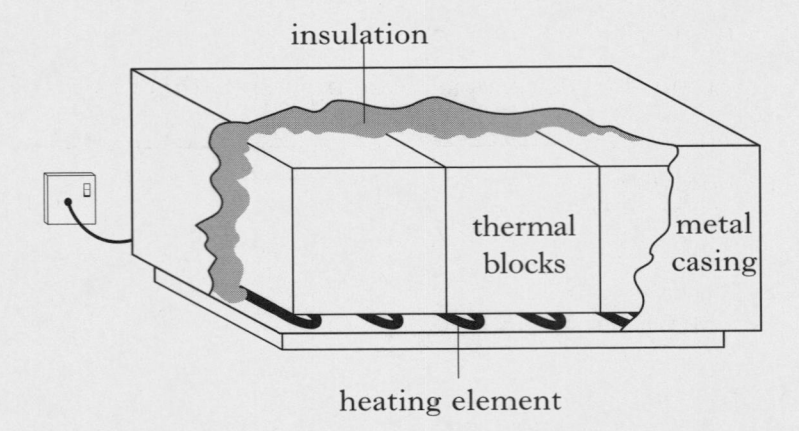

The heating element heats the thermal blocks during the night.

(a) Between midnight and 6.00 am, 8.64×10^7 J of energy are supplied to the heating element.

   (i) Calculate the power rating of the heating element.

   Space for working and answer

   (ii) The total mass of the thermal blocks in the heater is 144 kg and the specific heat capacity of the thermal blocks is 2625 J/kg °C.

   Calculate the maximum possible rise in the temperature of the thermal blocks between midnight and 6.00 am.

   Space for working and answer

10. *(a)* **(continued)**

    (iii) Explain why the actual temperature rise of the blocks is less than the value calculated in *(a)*(ii).

....

.... **1**

(b) Why is there insulation between the thermal blocks and the outer casing of the heater?

....

....

.... **1**

(c) During the day, heat energy stored in the heater is released into the room. State **one** way in which heat is transferred to the surroundings from this heater.

....

.... **1**

[Turn over

11. A refracting telescope has an objective lens which has a focal length of 800 mm and a diameter of 50 mm.

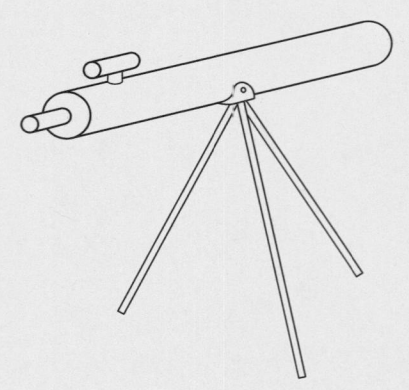

The telescope can be fitted with any one of three eyepiece lenses Q, R or S. Information on these lenses is shown in the table.

Lens	Focal length (mm)	Diameter (mm)
Q	10	5
R	20	5
S	40	5

(a) Why is it important to make the diameter of the **objective** lens as large as possible?

....

....

11. (continued)

(b) (i) Calculate the power of lens R.

Space for working and answer

2

(ii) Which of the three eyepiece lenses has the greatest power?

....

1

(c) Each eyepiece lens can be used on its own as a magnifying glass.

Complete the diagram below to show how lens S can be used to form a magnified image of an object.

The points marked F are one focal length from the centre of the lens.

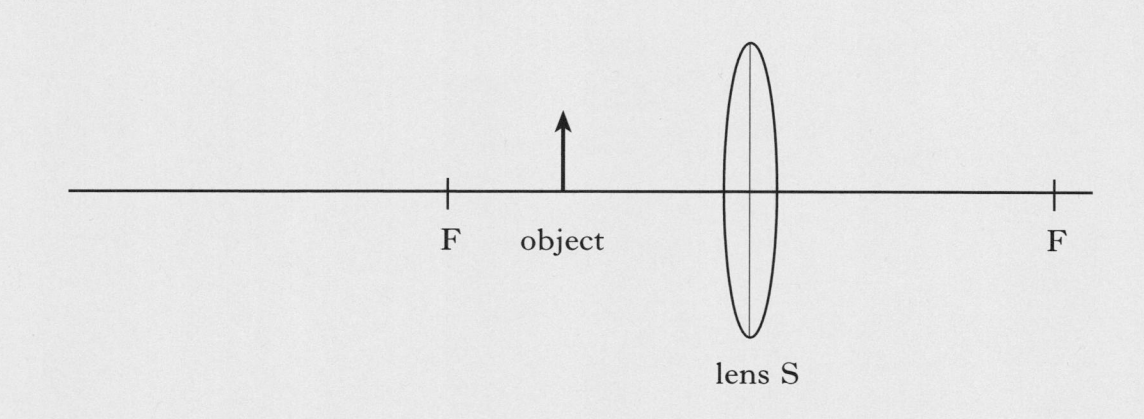

F   object   lens S   F

3

12. The International Space Station orbits Earth at a height of 360 km. The command module of the space station has a mass of 20 tonnes (20×10^3 kg).

(a) Masses as large as this are difficult to accelerate.

Circle the term that is used for this concept.

gravitational field strength   **inertia**   **thrust**   **weight**

(b) The graph shows how the gravitational field strength varies with height above the surface of the Earth.

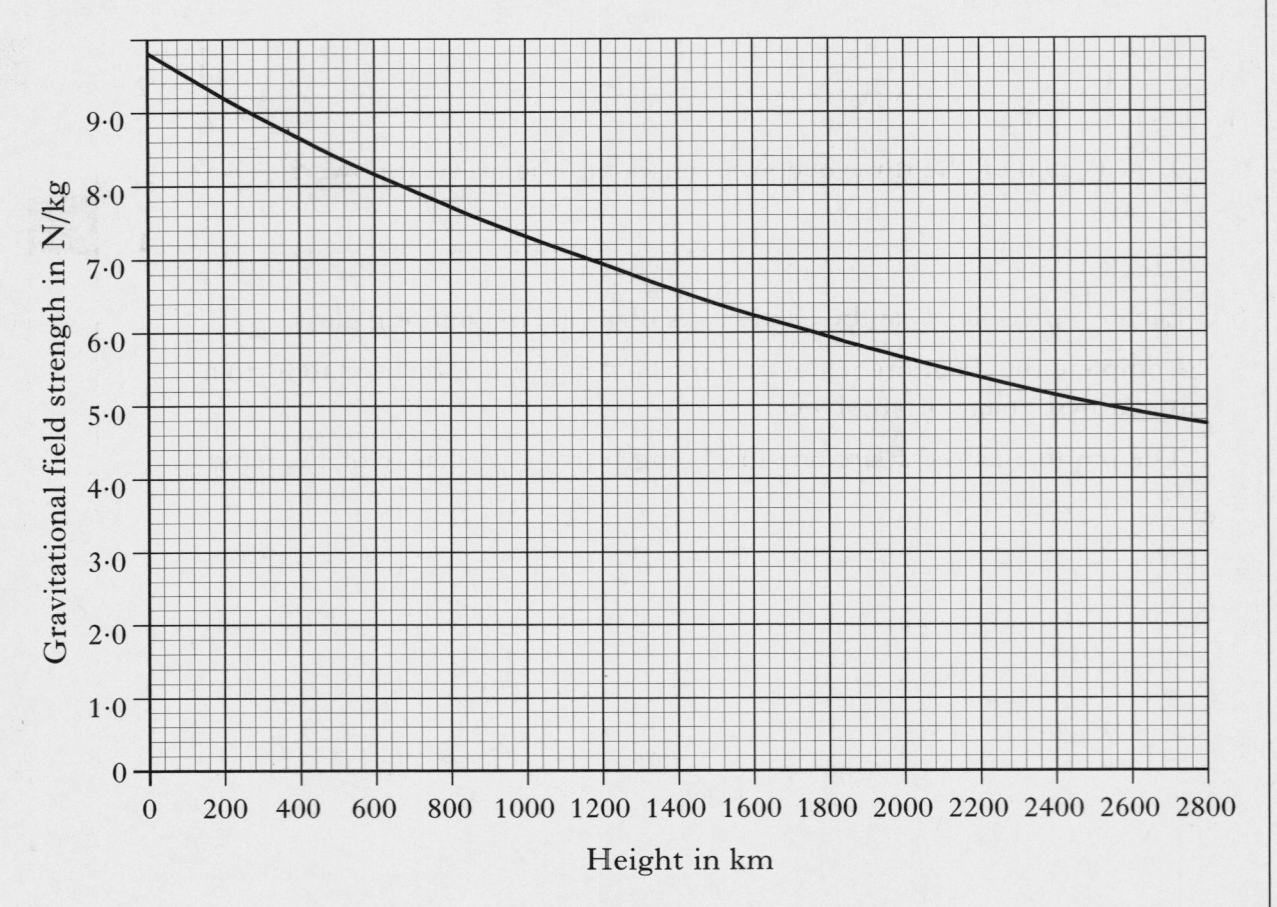

(i) What is the value of the gravitational field strength at the orbital height of the International Space Station?

....

12. **(b)** **(continued)**

   (ii) Calculate the weight of the command module at this height.

   Space for working and answer

   2

   (iii) As the command module is taken from Earth to its orbital height, what happens to its weight and mass?

   Weight ....

   Mass   2

(c) The International Space Station is an artificial satellite.

   Explain why it remains in orbit around the Earth.

   ....

   ....

   ....

     2

[*END OF QUESTION PAPER*]

YOU MAY USE THE SPACE ON THIS PAGE TO REWRITE ANY ANSWER YOU HAVE DECIDED TO CHANGE IN THE MAIN PART OF THE ANSWER BOOKLET. TAKE CARE TO WRITE IN CAREFULLY THE APPROPRIATE QUESTION NUMBER.

2001 CREDIT

Official SQA Past Papers: Credit Physics 2001

FOR OFFICIAL USE

C

K & U | PS

Total Marks

3220/402

NATIONAL QUALIFICATIONS 2001

MONDAY, 4 JUNE 10.50 AM – 12.35 PM

PHYSICS
STANDARD GRADE
Credit Level

Fill in these boxes and read what is printed below.

Full name of centre

Town

Forename(s)

Surname

Date of birth
Day Month Year

Scottish candidate number

Number of seat

1 All questions should be answered.

2 The questions may be answered in any order but all answers must be written clearly and legibly in this book.

3 Write your answer where indicated by the question or in the space provided after the question.

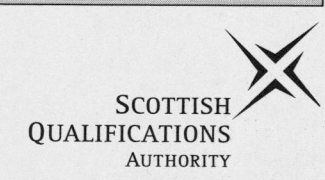

4 If you change your mind about your answer you may score it out and rewrite it in the space provided at the end of the answer book.

5 Before leaving the examination room you must give this book to the invigilator. If you do not, you may lose all the marks for this paper.

6 Any necessary data will be found in the **data sheet** on page two.

SCOTTISH
QUALIFICATIONS
AUTHORITY

LIB 3220/402 6/25820

DATA SHEET

Speed of light in materials

Material	Speed in m/s
Air	3.0×10^8
Carbon dioxide	3.0×10^8
Diamond	1.2×10^8
Glass	2.0×10^8
Glycerol	2.1×10^8
Water	2.3×10^8

Speed of sound in materials

Material	Speed in m/s
Aluminium	5200
Air	340
Bone	4100
Carbon dioxide	270
Glycerol	1900
Muscle	1600
Steel	5200
Tissue	1500
Water	1500

Gravitational field strengths

	Gravitational field strength on the surface in N/kg
Earth	10
Jupiter	26
Mars	4
Mercury	4
Moon	1.6
Neptune	12
Saturn	11
Sun	270
Venus	9

Specific heat capacity of materials

Material	Specific heat capacity in J/kg °C
Alcohol	2350
Aluminium	902
Copper	386
Diamond	530
Glass	500
Glycerol	2400
Ice	2100
Lead	128
Water	4180

Specific latent heat of fusion of materials

Material	Specific latent heat of fusion in J/kg
Alcohol	0.99×10^5
Aluminium	3.95×10^5
Carbon dioxide	1.80×10^5
Copper	2.05×10^5
Glycerol	1.81×10^5
Lead	0.25×10^5
Water	3.34×10^5

Melting and boiling points of materials

Material	Melting point in °C	Boiling point in °C
Alcohol	−98	65
Aluminium	660	2470
Copper	1077	2567
Glycerol	18	290
Lead	328	1737
Turpentine	−10	156

Specific latent heat of vaporisation of materials

Material	Specific latent heat of vaporisation in J/kg
Alcohol	11.2×10^5
Carbon dioxide	3.77×10^5
Glycerol	8.30×10^5
Turpentine	2.90×10^5
Water	22.6×10^5

SI Prefixes and Multiplication Factors

Prefix	Symbol	Factor	
giga	G	1 000 000 000	$= 10^9$
mega	M	1 000 000	$= 10^6$
kilo	k	1000	$= 10^3$
milli	m	0.001	$= 10^{-3}$
micro	μ	0.000 001	$= 10^{-6}$
nano	n	0.000 000 001	$= 10^{-9}$

1. The depth of the seabed is measured using pulses of ultrasound waves. The ultrasound waves are transmitted from a stationary ship. The waves are reflected from the seabed as shown and are detected by equipment on the ship. The transmitted ultrasound waves have a frequency of 30 kHz.

(a) One pulse of ultrasound waves is received back at the ship 0·2 s after being sent out.

   (i) Use the data sheet to find the speed of the ultrasound waves in the water.

....

   (ii) Calculate the depth of the seabed.

Space for working and answer

   (iii) Calculate the wavelength of the ultrasound waves in the water.

Space for working and answer

[Turn over

1. (continued)

(b) The ultrasound waves lose energy as they travel through the water. The transmitted wave is displayed on an oscilloscope screen as shown.

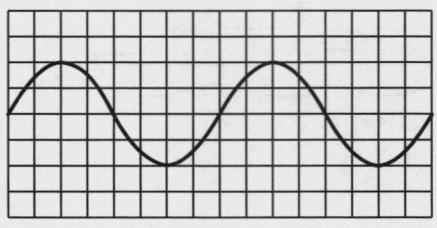

Transmitted

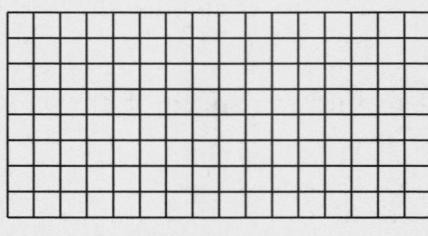

Reflected

On the bottom part of the diagram, sketch the trace produced by the reflected wave.

2

(c) The frequency of the transmitted wave is increased to 60 kHz.

What happens to the time interval between the transmitted pulse and the reflected pulse?

Explain your answer.

....

....

....

....

2

2. A mobile phone has a power of 75 mW and operates using a 3 V battery.

   (a) Calculate the current taken from the battery when the mobile phone is being used.

   Space for working and answer

   (b) Which of the following fuses should be connected in series with the battery of the mobile phone?

   20 mA   **100 mA**   **2 A**   **3 A**

   ....

   [Turn over

3. A 2·5 V, 100 mA lamp is operated at its correct power rating from a 12 V battery by using the circuit shown.

12 V battery

(a) A voltmeter and an ammeter included in the circuit show that the lamp is operating at its correct rating.

Enter the readings that are seen on the meters. Include the units for both readings.

(b) (i) Calculate the voltage across the resistor.

Space for working and answer

(ii) Calculate the resistance of the resistor.

Space for working and answer

4. A simple d.c. motor is shown in Figure 1.

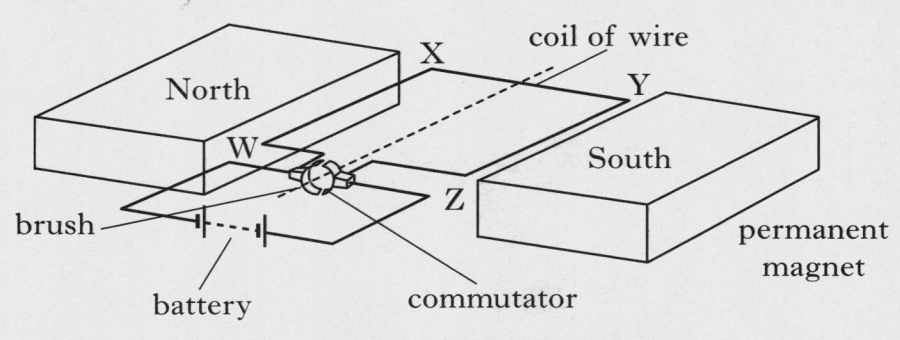

Figure 1

(a) The coil WXYZ rotates in a clockwise direction.

State **two** changes that could be made to make the coil rotate in the opposite direction.

Change 1 ....

....

Change 2 ....

....

[Turn over

4. (continued)

(b) Part of a commercial electric motor is shown in Figure 2.

Figure 2

(i) Label the two parts indicated on the motor, using names from the list below.

brush   commutator   field coil   rotating coil

(ii) In the commercial electric motor, state why

(A) more than one rotating coil is used

....

....

(B) field coils rather than permanent magnets are used.

....

....

5. (*a*) A long-sighted person is prescribed glasses that have lenses each with a power of 2·5 D.

    (i) State what is meant by long-sight.

    ....

    ....

    (ii) Calculate the focal length of each lens.

Space for working and answer

(*b*) Complete the diagram below to show the path of the ray of light after it emerges from the lens.

lens

[Turn over

6. Carbon dating is used by scientists to tell the age of organic (formerly living) material. This method is based on knowing that the half-life of radioactive carbon is 5730 years.

(a) Explain what is meant by the statement "the half-life of radioactive carbon is 5730 years".

....

....

(b) The proportion of radioactive carbon in the organic material is found by measuring its activity using a scintillation counter.

(i) State the **unit** that is used for the activity of a radioactive source.

....

(ii) Describe how a scintillation counter is used as a detector of radiation.

....

....

....

(iii) State an example of the effect of radiation other than scintillations.

....

7. A thermistor is used as a temperature sensor in the voltage divider circuit shown below. The circuit is used to sense the temperature of water in a tank. When the temperature of the water in the tank falls below a certain value, the output of the voltage divider causes a switching circuit to operate a heater.

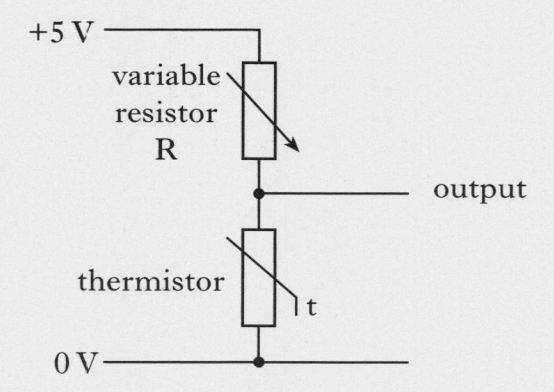

(a) When the voltage across the thermistor reaches 0·7 V, the circuit causes the heater to be switched on.

(i) The variable resistor R is set to a resistance of 4300 Ω.

Calculate the resistance of the thermistor when the voltage across the thermistor is 0·7 V.

Space for working and answer

[Turn over

7. (a) (continued)

(ii) The graph shows how the resistance of the thermistor changes with temperature.

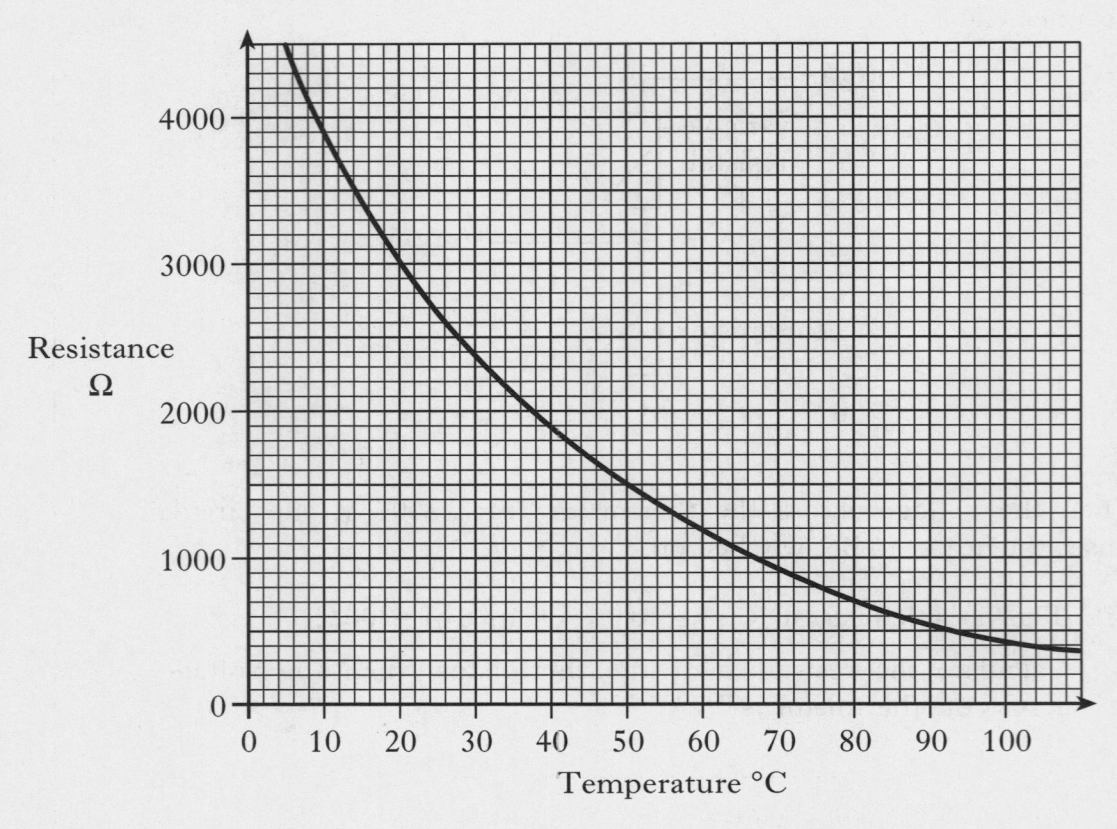

[Graph of Resistance Ω vs Temperature °C, showing a decreasing curve from about 4500 Ω at low temperature to about 400 Ω at 100 °C]

(A) Use the graph to decide the temperature at which the heater is switched on.

....

(B) The resistance of the variable resistor R is increased to a value **greater than** 4300 Ω.

What effect does this have on the temperature at which the heater is switched on?

Explain your answer.

....

....

....

7. (continued)

(b) The voltage divider circuit is connected to the switching circuit, as shown, to operate the heater. When there is a current in the relay coil, the relay switch closes.

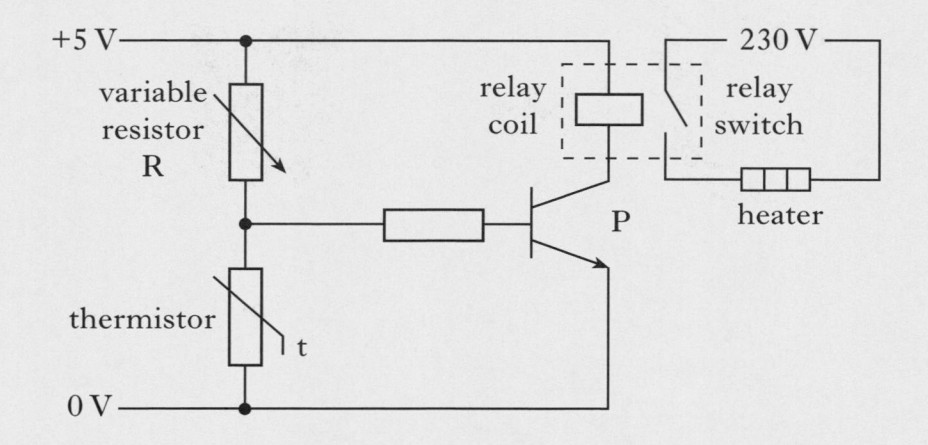

(i) Name component P.

....

(ii) Explain why the heater switches on as the temperature falls below a selected value.

....

....

....

....

....

[Turn over

8. An electric guitar is connected to an amplifier.

The input power to the amplifier from the guitar is 16 mW. The output of the amplifier is connected to a loudspeaker. The loudspeaker has a resistance of 9 Ω.

(a) The amplifier delivers an output power of 64 W to the loudspeaker.

   (i) Calculate the power gain of the amplifier.

   Space for working and answer

   (ii) Calculate the voltage across the loudspeaker.

   Space for working and answer

8. (continued)

(b) A second, identical loudspeaker is connected in parallel with the first.

Calculate the combined resistance of the two loudspeakers in parallel.

Space for working and answer

(c) The guitarist plays a note of frequency 256 Hz.

What is the frequency of the output signal from the amplifier?

....

[Turn over

9. A cyclist has a small computer attached to her bike. The computer gives information on the cyclist's instantaneous speed, distance travelled and time taken.

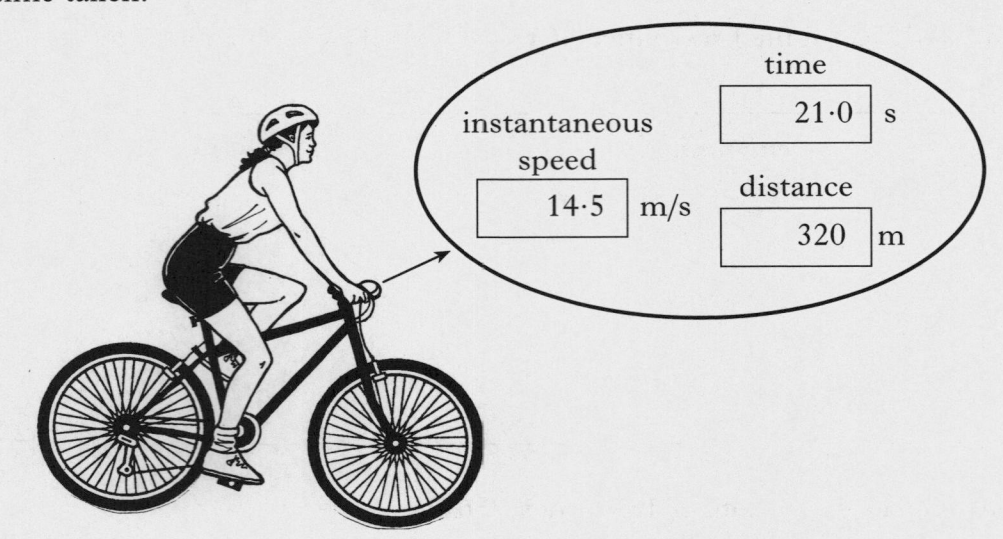

time: 21·0 s
instantaneous speed: 14·5 m/s
distance: 320 m

At a point during a journey, the readings on the display are as shown above.

(a) (i) Calculate the average speed of the cyclist up to this point.

(You must use an appropriate number of significant figures in your answer to this question.)

Space for working and answer

(ii) Why is the average speed of the cyclist not always the same as the instantaneous speed displayed on the computer?

9. (continued)

(b) (i) The total mass of the cyclist and bike is 80 kg.

Calculate the total kinetic energy of the cyclist and the bike at this point during the journey.

Space for working and answer

2

(ii) The cyclist brakes to a halt in a distance of 50 m.

Calculate the braking force used.

Space for working and answer

2

[Turn over

10. An aircraft has a mass of 268 000 kg. The aircraft accelerates from rest along a straight runway. It takes 40 s for the aircraft to reach its take-off speed of 80 m/s.

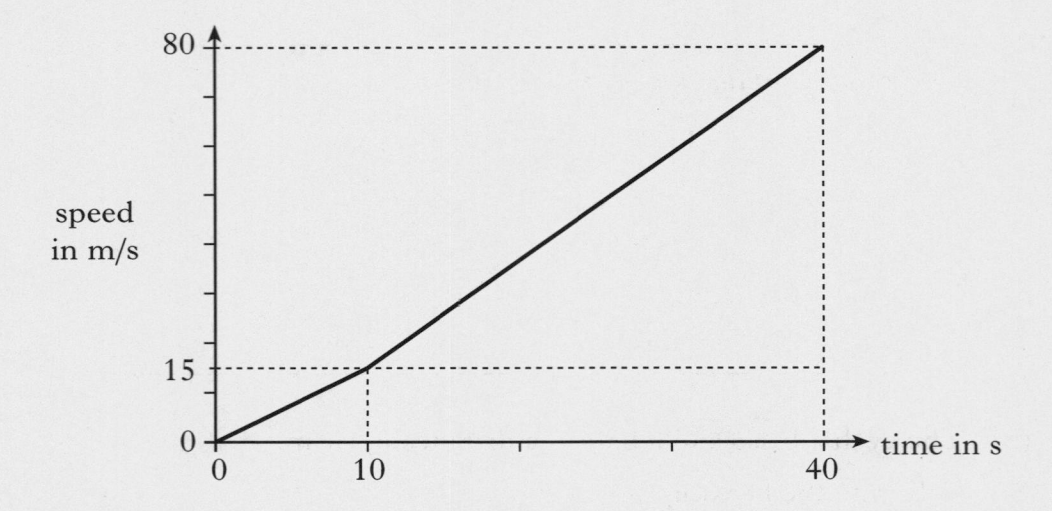

(a) The speed-time graph of the aircraft is shown.

(i) Calculate the acceleration of the aircraft **during the first 10 s**.

Space for working and answer

(ii) Calculate the unbalanced force acting on the aircraft **during the first 10 s**.

Space for working and answer

10. (*a*) (**continued**)

    (iii) By using information **from the graph**, explain whether the unbalanced force on the aircraft is greater during the time period 0–10 s or 10 s–40 s.

....

....

....

    (iv) Calculate the length of runway required to allow the aircraft to reach its take-off speed.

Space for working and answer

(*b*) After take-off, the aircraft flies at a constant height of 10 000 m. The pilot increases the speed of the aircraft at this height.

The diagram shows the forces acting on the aircraft at this height.

Complete the statements about the sizes of the forces acting on the aircraft by using phrases from the following list.

    equal to   **greater than**   **less than**

  (i) The engine thrust is................................. the air friction force.

  (ii) The lift is........................... the weight.

11. (a) The following information relates to two power stations, a fossil fuel power station and a nuclear power station.

Fossil Fuel Power Station	**Nuclear Power Station**
Heat energy produced per kilogram of fuel $4 \cdot 5 \times 10^7$ J	Heat energy produced per kilogram of fuel $4 \cdot 4 \times 10^{11}$ J
Waste produced per year —not radioactive 100 000 kg	Waste produced per year —radioactive 5 kg
Cooling water required 550 kg/s	Cooling water required 550 kg/s

(i) Compare the information given for the two types of power station. State **one** advantage of generating electricity using each type of power station.

Fossil fuel ....

....

Nuclear ....

....

(ii) Using information given, state where both types of power station are likely to be located.

Explain why they are built in these locations.

....

....

....

(b) A simple block diagram of a nuclear power station is shown below.

Reactor core → Turbine → Generator

State the energy transformation that takes place in

(i) the reactor core

....

(ii) the generator.

....

11. (continued)

(c) The diagram shows what happens when a uranium nucleus undergoes fission in a nuclear reaction.

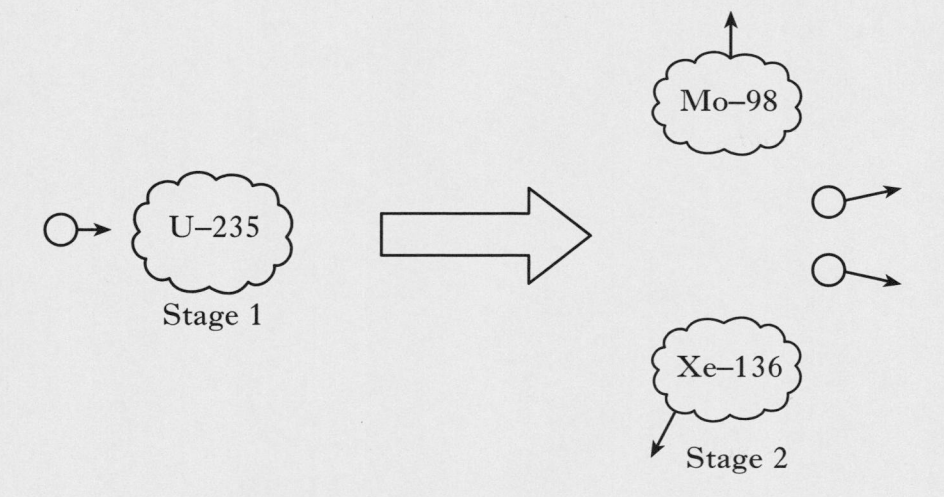

(i) Circle **one** word in each set of brackets to describe what happens at each stage.

Stage 1: A uranium nucleus is bombarded by a $\begin{Bmatrix} \text{proton} \\ \text{neutron} \\ \text{electron} \end{Bmatrix}$.

Stage 2: The uranium nucleus disintegrates, producing fission fragments, two $\begin{Bmatrix} \text{protons} \\ \text{neutrons} \\ \text{electrons} \end{Bmatrix}$ and $\begin{Bmatrix} \text{plutonium} \\ \text{heat} \\ \text{electricity} \end{Bmatrix}$.

3

(ii) Describe how, in a nuclear reactor, the above process can result in a chain reaction.

....

....

....

3

[Turn over

12. Ice cubes are used to cool down water for drinking. Each ice cube has a mass of 12 g and is initially at a temperature of 0 °C.

(a) Calculate how much heat is needed to melt an ice cube.

(Any additional information needed can be found in the data sheet on page 2.)

Space for working and answer

(b) When an ice cube is added to water, where does most of the energy come from to melt the ice?

....

(c) (i) An ice cube is added to a glass containing 200 g of water.

The initial temperature of the water is 18 °C. The final temperature when all of the ice has melted is 15 °C.

Calculate the heat removed from the water.

(Any additional information needed can be found in the data sheet on page 2.)

Space for working and answer

(ii) Suggest a final temperature when an ice cube is added to an insulated bottle of water. The bottle has a lid and contains an equal mass of water as above, and is at the same initial temperature.

Explain your answer.

....

....

....

13. Read the following passage about the launching of a space observatory using the Space Shuttle Columbia.

In July 1999, NASA used the Space Shuttle Columbia to launch a space-based observatory, called the Chandra X-ray Observatory.

This observatory is designed to detect X-rays emitted by objects in our solar system and beyond. X-rays are absorbed by the Earth's atmosphere, so a space-based observatory is necessary to detect them. Signals are sent from the observatory to Earth using radio waves.

There are now three observatories orbiting the Earth. The other two are the Hubble Space Telescope that detects visible light and the Compton Gamma Ray Observatory.

(a) Why is it necessary to site an observatory in space to detect X-rays?

....

....

(b) Four members of the electromagnetic spectrum are mentioned in the passage. Complete the diagram by placing these members in the correct order of wavelength.

		Ultraviolet		Infrared	Microwaves	

The electromagnetic spectrum

(c) Explain why different kinds of observatory are used to detect signals from space.

....

....

....

[Turn over

13. (continued)

(d) When the Space Shuttle reached the correct height above Earth, the observatory was separated from it.

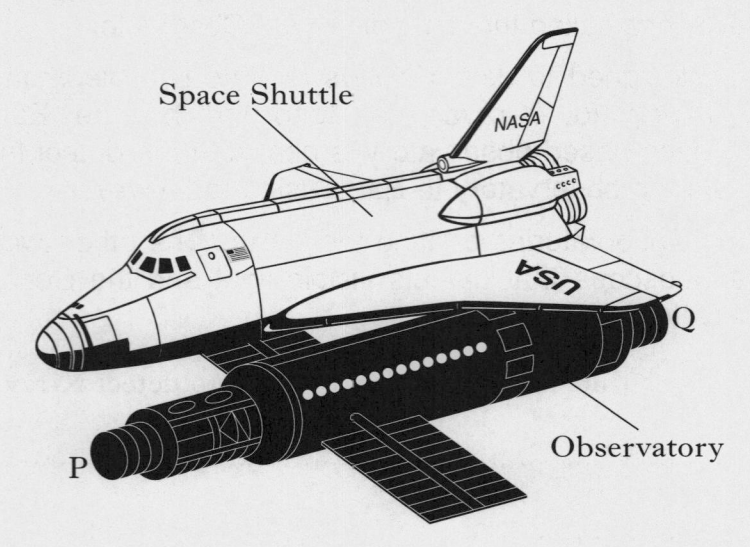

Two rocket motors P and Q on the observatory, as shown, were used during the separation. The observatory accelerated away from the space shuttle for a short time. It then remained at a fixed distance ahead of the space shuttle. Describe how the rockets P and Q were used during this separation.

....

....

....

....

2

[END OF QUESTION PAPER]

2002 CREDIT

Official SQA Past Papers: Credit Physics 2002

FOR OFFICIAL USE

C

K & U   PS

Total Marks

3220/402

NATIONAL QUALIFICATIONS 2002

MONDAY, 27 MAY 10.50 AM – 12.35 PM

PHYSICS
STANDARD GRADE
Credit Level

Fill in these boxes and read what is printed below.

Full name of centre

Town

Forename(s)

Surname

Date of birth
Day Month Year   Scottish candidate number   Number of seat

1. All questions should be answered.

2. The questions may be answered in any order but all answers must be written clearly and legibly in this book.

3. Write your answer where indicated by the question or in the space provided after the question.

4. If you change your mind about your answer you may score it out and rewrite it in the space provided at the end of the answer book.

5. Before leaving the examination room you must give this book to the invigilator. If you do not, you may lose all the marks for this paper.

6. Any necessary data will be found in the **data sheet** on page two.

SCOTTISH QUALIFICATIONS AUTHORITY

DATA SHEET

Speed of light in materials

Material	Speed in m/s
Air	3.0×10^8
Carbon dioxide	3.0×10^8
Diamond	1.2×10^8
Glass	2.0×10^8
Glycerol	2.1×10^8
Water	2.3×10^8

Speed of sound in materials

Material	Speed in m/s
Aluminium	5200
Air	340
Bone	4100
Carbon dioxide	270
Glycerol	1900
Muscle	1600
Steel	5200
Tissue	1500
Water	1500

Gravitational field strengths

	Gravitational field strength on the surface in N/kg
Earth	10
Jupiter	26
Mars	4
Mercury	4
Moon	1.6
Neptune	12
Saturn	11
Sun	270
Venus	9

Specific heat capacity of materials

Material	Specific heat capacity in J/kg °C
Alcohol	2350
Aluminium	902
Copper	386
Diamond	530
Glass	500
Glycerol	2400
Ice	2100
Lead	128
Water	4180

Specific latent heat of fusion of materials

Material	Specific latent heat of fusion in J/kg
Alcohol	0.99×10^5
Aluminium	3.95×10^5
Carbon dioxide	1.80×10^5
Copper	2.05×10^5
Glycerol	1.81×10^5
Lead	0.25×10^5
Water	3.34×10^5

Melting and boiling points of materials

Material	Melting point in °C	Boiling point in °C
Alcohol	−98	65
Aluminium	660	2470
Copper	1077	2567
Glycerol	18	290
Lead	328	1737
Turpentine	−10	156

Specific latent heat of vaporisation of materials

Material	Specific latent heat of vaporisation in J/kg
Alcohol	11.2×10^5
Carbon dioxide	3.77×10^5
Glycerol	8.30×10^5
Turpentine	2.90×10^5
Water	22.6×10^5

SI Prefixes and Multiplication Factors

Prefix	Symbol	Factor	
giga	G	1 000 000 000	$= 10^9$
mega	M	1 000 000	$= 10^6$
kilo	k	1000	$= 10^3$
milli	m	0.001	$= 10^{-3}$
micro	μ	0.000 001	$= 10^{-6}$
nano	n	0.000 000 001	$= 10^{-9}$

1. Radio Alba transmits on a range of frequencies from different transmitters throughout Scotland.

On a car journey from Aberdeen to Stirling a driver listens to Radio Alba. At the start of the journey she tunes to the signal transmitted from transmitter P.

(a) Complete the following passage, using some of the words from the list below. Do not use any word more than once.

amplitude audio carrier
frequency modulation radio

The transmitter transmits a ....radio................ signal, which consists of an ....audio................ wave and a ....carrier................ wave. The process of combining these waves is known as ....modulation................ .

(b) During the journey the driver finds that the signal from transmitter P fades.

(i) Suggest a reason why the signal fades.

....

....

(ii) To continue to listen to Radio Alba, the driver re-tunes the radio to pick up the signal from transmitter Q.

What is the difference between the carrier wave from transmitter P and that from transmitter Q?

....

....

2. The table gives information about artificial satellites that orbit the Earth.

Name of satellite	Period (minutes)	Height above Earth (km)	Use
Landsat	99	705	Land mapping
ERS-1		780	Monitoring sea levels
NOAA-12	102	833	Distribution of ozone layer
Early Bird	1440	35 900	Continuous telecommunication

(a) NOAA-12 uses radio waves to transmit signals relating to the ozone layer.

   (i) What is the speed of radio waves?

   ....

   (ii) Calculate the time for signals to travel from NOAA-12 to an Earth station immediately below the satellite.

   Space for working and answer

   (iii) Signals transmitted from NOAA-12 have a frequency of 137·5 MHz.

   Calculate the wavelength of these signals.

   Space for working and answer

2. **(continued)**

   (b) Using information about the period of Early Bird, explain why this satellite is used for continuous telecommunication between two points on the Earth's surface.

   ....

   ....

   2

   (c) Give an approximate value, **in minutes**, for the period of orbit of ERS-1.

   1

   (d) Landsat monitors heat emission from the land to build up a thermographic image.

   Which part of the electromagnetic spectrum is detected by Landsat?

   1

   (e) As well as artificial satellites, there is one natural satellite that orbits the Earth. Name this natural satellite.

   1

   [Turn over

3. A student uses the circuit below in experiments to investigate how the voltage across different components varies when the current in the components is changed.

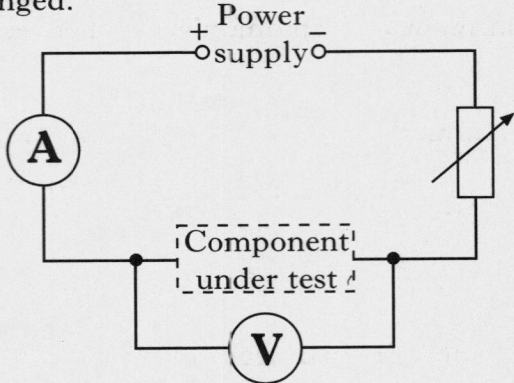

(a) The student places component X in the circuit and carries out an experiment. The graph below shows how the voltage across component X varies with current.

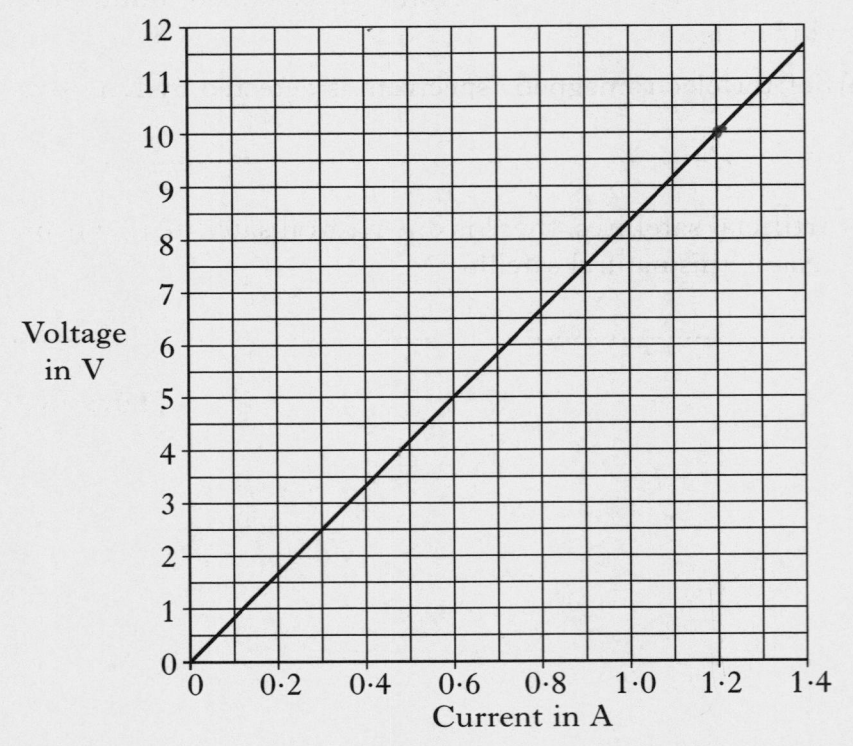

(i) Calculate the resistance of component X when the current is 1·2 A.

(You must use an appropriate number of significant figures in your answer to this question.)

Space for working and answer

3. *(a)* **(continued)**

(ii) Using information from the graph, explain what happens to the resistance of component X as the current is increased.

Justify your answer by calculation or otherwise.

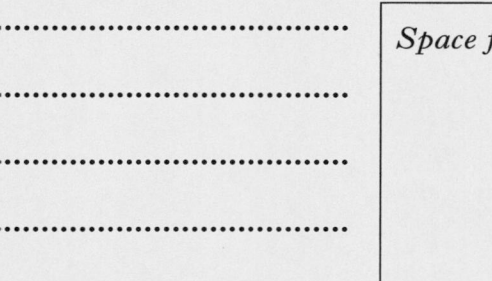

....

Space for working

(b) The student replaces component X with component Y, repeats the experiment and obtains the following graph.

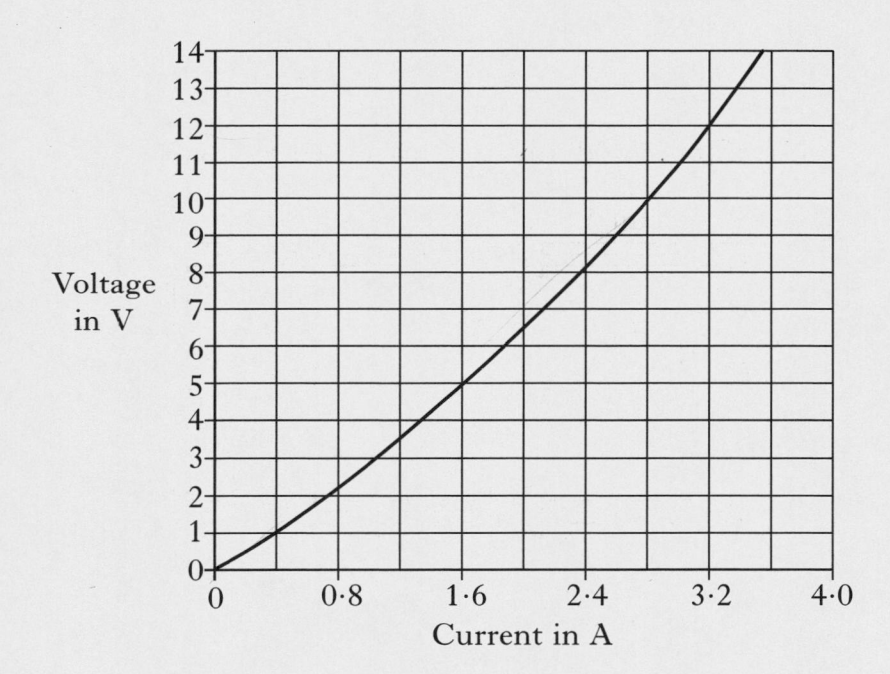

(i) The student concludes that the resistance of component Y is not constant. Why is the student correct in coming to this conclusion?

clearly because the graph line is not in a straight line.

[Turn over

3. (b) (continued)

(ii) (A) From the graph, what is the current in component Y when the voltage across component Y is 12 V?

...... 3.2 A ......

(B) Calculate the power dissipated in component Y when the voltage across it is 12 V.

Space for working and answer

P = IV
P = ?
I = 3.2
V = 12

P = IV
P = 3.2 × 12
P = 38.4 W

4. The diagram shows three household circuits, connected to a consumer unit.

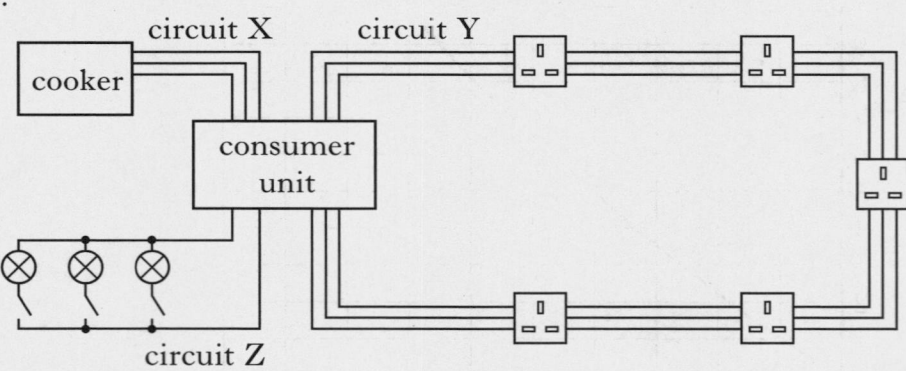

(a) (i) Which circuit is a ring circuit?

...... Circuit Y ......

(ii) Give **two** advantages of using a ring circuit.

...... less heat, cheaper wires because it splits up. ......

4. (continued)

(b) State and explain **one** difference between a lighting circuit and a ring circuit.

the lighting circuit uses thinner cables so lower current

(c) (i) Why does a cooker need a separate circuit?

because it produces heat it has a larger current

(ii) One heating element of the cooker has a power rating of 2·2 kW. Calculate how many joules of energy are transferred by this element in 2 hours.

Space for working and answer

P = E/T
P = 2200   E = 2200 × 120
E = ?   E =
T = 120

(d) (i) What is the purpose of an earth wire?

to prevent electrocution

(ii) Explain how an earth wire works.

provides a path to ground (0v) so that if a large current is drawn, it will go to 0V.

[Turn over

5. Ultrasound is used by doctors for treatment and diagnosis.

(a) Pulses of ultrasound are used to produce local heating of muscle deep inside the body. This heating effect can help relieve pain in the muscles.

(i) What is meant by ultrasound?

...... high frequency sounds ......

(ii) Calculate the time for a pulse of ultrasound to travel through 2 cm of muscle.

(Data you require will be found in the Data Sheet on *page two*.)

Space for working and answer

t =

(b) Ultrasound is also used to build up images of an unborn baby.

(i) Explain how ultrasound is used to build up such images.

(ii) Why is ultrasound safer than X-rays for this sort of medical application?

6. A student investigates the effect of glass shapes on rays of light.

(a) The student places glass shapes in the path of three rays of red light as shown.

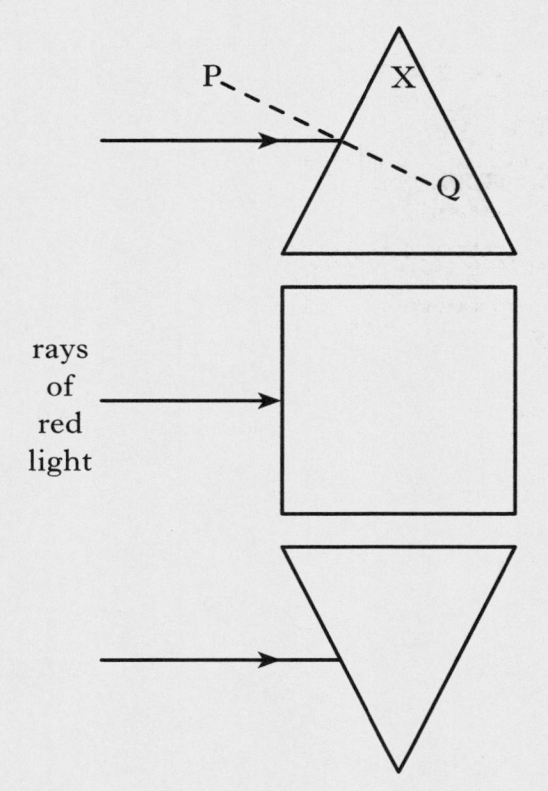

(i) Complete the diagram to show the paths of the rays of light through and out of the three glass shapes. **3**

(ii) The student has drawn line PQ on the diagram at shape X at right angles to the glass surface.

What name is given to this line?

.... **1**

(iii) **On the diagram**, label **one** angle of incidence as *i* and **one** angle of refraction as *r*. **2**

(b) Name the type of lens that would have a similar effect on the rays of light as the three glass shapes, arranged as in part (a).

.... **1**

[Turn over

7. The exit of an underground car park has an automatic barrier. The barrier rises when a car interrupts a light beam across the exit and money has been put into the pay machine. The barrier can also be operated by using a manual switch.

The light beam is directed at an LDR that is connected as shown in the circuit below.

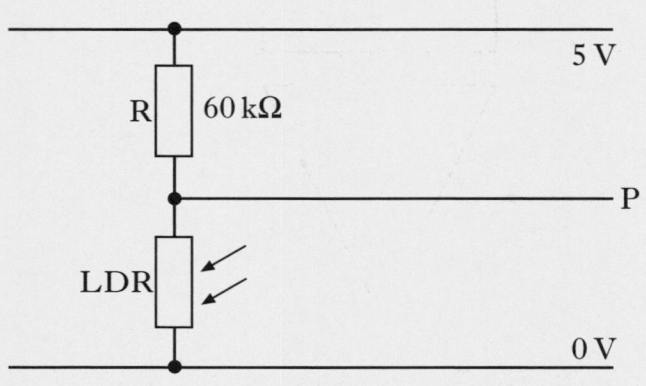

(a) Calculate the voltage across the LDR when its resistance is $15\,k\Omega$.

Space for working and answer

7. (continued)

(b) Part of the control circuit for the automatic barrier is shown below.

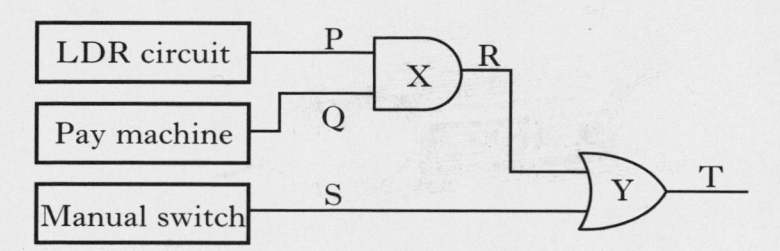

When a car interrupts the light beam, the logic level at P changes from logic 0 to logic 1.

When money is put into the pay machine, the logic level at Q changes from logic 0 to logic 1.

When the manual switch is operated, the logic level at S changes from logic 0 to logic 1.

(i) Name logic gate X.

.... 1

(ii) Name logic gate Y.

.... 1

(iii) Complete the truth table below for the control circuit shown, by filling in the values of the logic levels at R and T.

P	Q	R	S	T
0	0		0	
0	1		0	
1	0		0	
1	1		0	
0	0		1	
0	1		1	
1	0		1	
1	1		1	

4

(iv) Describe a situation where it would be necessary to operate the barrier by using the manual switch.

....

.... 1

[Turn over

8. A radio has three types of output device.

filament lamp **LED** **loudspeaker**

(a) Which of these output devices transforms electrical energy into sound energy?

....

(b) Which of these output devices is most suitable for illuminating the front panel of the radio?

Explain your choice.

....

....

....

(c) The LED is connected in series with resistor, R, to the 9·0 V power supply of the radio.

(i) In the space in the circuit above draw the LED connected correctly.

(ii) When lit, the voltage across the LED is 2·4 V and the current in the LED is 20 mA.

Calculate the resistance of R.

Space for working and answer

9. A skateboarder is practising on a ramp. The total mass of the skateboarder and the board is 60 kg.

(a) Calculate the increase in potential energy of the skateboarder and board in moving from the ground to position P.

Space for working and answer

(b) The skateboarder moves along the ramp from P to R, and rises into the air above R.

  (i) At what point **on the ramp** is the kinetic energy of the skateboarder greatest?

  ....

  (ii) The vertical speed of the skateboarder at R is 6 m/s.
  Calculate the height that the skateboarder rises to, above R.

  Space for working and answer

  (iii) Explain why the skateboarder does not rise to the same height as P.

  ....
  ....
  ....

10. At a greyhound racing track, the greyhounds are automatically released when an artificial hare crosses the starting line.

The speed-time graph shows the motion of one greyhound and the hare from the time when the hare crosses the starting line.

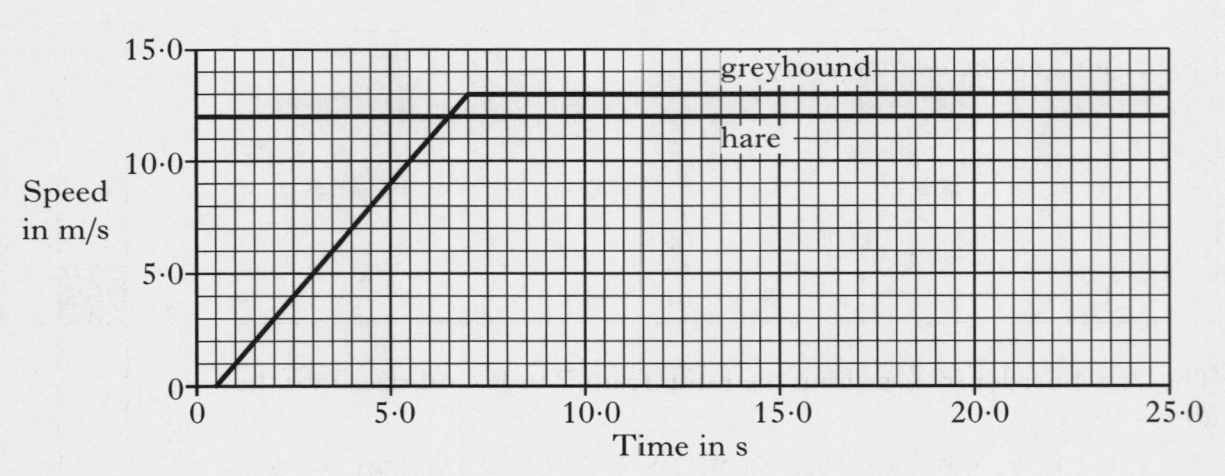

(a) How long does it take for the greyhound to start moving after the hare crosses the starting line?

....

(b) Calculate the acceleration of the greyhound when it starts moving.

Space for working and answer

10. (continued)

(c) The hare crosses the finishing line 20 s after crossing the starting line.

   (i) Over what distance is the race run?

   Space for working and answer

   2

   (ii) How far behind the hare is the greyhound when the **hare** finishes the race?

   Space for working and answer

   3

[**Turn over**

11. A lighting system in a shop window uses three identical 18 W, 12 V filament lamps. The lamps are operated at their correct rating from the 230 V mains supply using a transformer as shown below.

There are 5750 turns on the primary coil of the transformer.

(a) Calculate the number of turns on the secondary coil of the transformer.

Space for working and answer

(b) (i) The current in each lamp is 1·5 A.

Calculate the total current in the secondary circuit of the transformer.

Space for working and answer

(ii) Assuming that the transformer is 100% efficient, calculate the current in the primary coil.

Space for working and answer

11. (continued)

(c) (i) Show that the resistance of one of the filament lamps, when it is operating normally, is $8 \cdot 0 \, \Omega$.

Space for working and answer

2

(ii) Calculate the combined resistance of the three lamps in parallel.

Space for working and answer

2

[Turn over

12. A student sets up the apparatus shown to measure the specific heat capacity of an aluminium block.

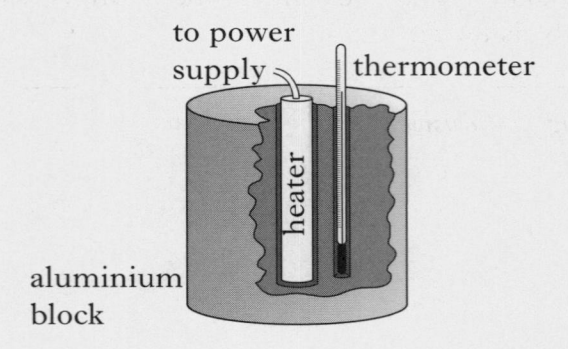

[Diagram: aluminium block with heater connected to power supply and thermometer inserted]

The student obtains the following results:

mass of aluminium block $m = 0.8$ kg
temperature change $\Delta T = 19\,°C$
time taken $t = 5.0$ minutes
heater current $I = 4.2$ A
heater voltage $V = 12$ V

(a) Show, by calculation, that 15 120 J of electrical energy are supplied to the heater in 5·0 minutes.

Space for working and answer

(b) (i) Assuming all of the electrical energy is transferred to the aluminium block as heat energy, calculate the value of the specific heat capacity of aluminium obtained from this experiment.

Space for working and answer

12. (b) (continued)

(ii) The accepted value of the specific heat capacity of aluminium is 902 J/kg °C.

(A) Give a reason for the difference between your answer in (b)(i) and this value.

....

....

....

(B) How could the experiment be improved to reduce this difference?

....

....

....

[Turn over

13. During the Apollo 11 expedition to the Moon, 21 kg of soil samples were brought from the Moon to the Earth. The gravitational field strength was not constant throughout the journey.

(a) What is meant by gravitational field strength?

....

....

(b) Complete the table to show the mass and weight of the soil samples at various stages of the journey.

Stage	Gravitational field strength (N/kg)	Mass (kg)	Weight (N)
on the Moon	1·6	21	
at a point during the journey	0		
on the Earth	10		

[END OF QUESTION PAPER]

2003 CREDIT

Official SQA Past Papers: Credit Physics 2003

FOR OFFICIAL USE

C

K & U   PS

Total Marks

3220/402

NATIONAL
QUALIFICATIONS
2003

MONDAY, 19 MAY
10.50 AM – 12.35 PM

**PHYSICS
STANDARD GRADE**
Credit Level

Fill in these boxes and read what is printed below.

Full name of centre

Town

Forename(s)

I'm Gonna

Surname

Fail

Date of birth
Day Month Year

Scottish candidate number

I dontknow

Number of seat

1 All questions should be answered.

2 The questions may be answered in any order but all answers must be written clearly and legibly in this book.

3 Write your answer where indicated by the question or in the space provided after the question.

4 If you change your mind about your answer you may score it out and rewrite it in the space provided at the end of the answer book.

5 Before leaving the examination room you must give this book to the invigilator. If you do not, you may lose all the marks for this paper.

6 Any necessary data will be found in the **data sheet** on page two.

SCOTTISH
QUALIFICATIONS
AUTHORITY

SAB 3220/402
6/3/3/25870

DATA SHEET

Speed of light in materials

Material	Speed in m/s
Air	3.0×10^8
Carbon dioxide	3.0×10^8
Diamond	1.2×10^8
Glass	2.0×10^8
Glycerol	2.1×10^8
Water	2.3×10^8

Speed of sound in materials

Material	Speed in m/s
Aluminium	5200
Air	340
Bone	4100
Carbon dioxide	270
Glycerol	1900
Muscle	1600
Steel	5200
Tissue	1500
Water	1500

Gravitational field strengths

	Gravitational field strength on the surface in N/kg
Earth	10
Jupiter	26
Mars	4
Mercury	4
Moon	1.6
Neptune	12
Saturn	11
Sun	270
Venus	9

Specific heat capacity of materials

Material	Specific heat capacity in J/kg °C
Alcohol	2350
Aluminium	902
Copper	386
Diamond	530
Glass	500
Glycerol	2400
Ice	2100
Lead	128
Water	4180

Specific latent heat of fusion of materials

Material	Specific latent heat of fusion in J/kg
Alcohol	0.99×10^5
Aluminium	3.95×10^5
Carbon dioxide	1.80×10^5
Copper	2.05×10^5
Glycerol	1.81×10^5
Lead	0.25×10^5
Water	3.34×10^5

Melting and boiling points of materials

Material	Melting point in °C	Boiling point in °C
Alcohol	−98	65
Aluminium	660	2470
Copper	1077	2567
Glycerol	18	290
Lead	328	1737
Turpentine	−10	156

Specific latent heat of vaporisation of materials

Material	Specific latent heat of vaporisation in J/kg
Alcohol	11.2×10^5
Carbon dioxide	3.77×10^5
Glycerol	8.30×10^5
Turpentine	2.90×10^5
Water	22.6×10^5

SI Prefixes and Multiplication Factors

Prefix	Symbol	Factor	
giga	G	1 000 000 000	$= 10^9$
mega	M	1 000 000	$= 10^6$
kilo	k	1000	$= 10^3$
milli	m	0.001	$= 10^{-3}$
micro	μ	0.000 001	$= 10^{-6}$
nano	n	0.000 000 001	$= 10^{-9}$

1. A farm road joins a main road at a bend. The farmer has placed a mirror as shown so that he can see when cars are approaching.

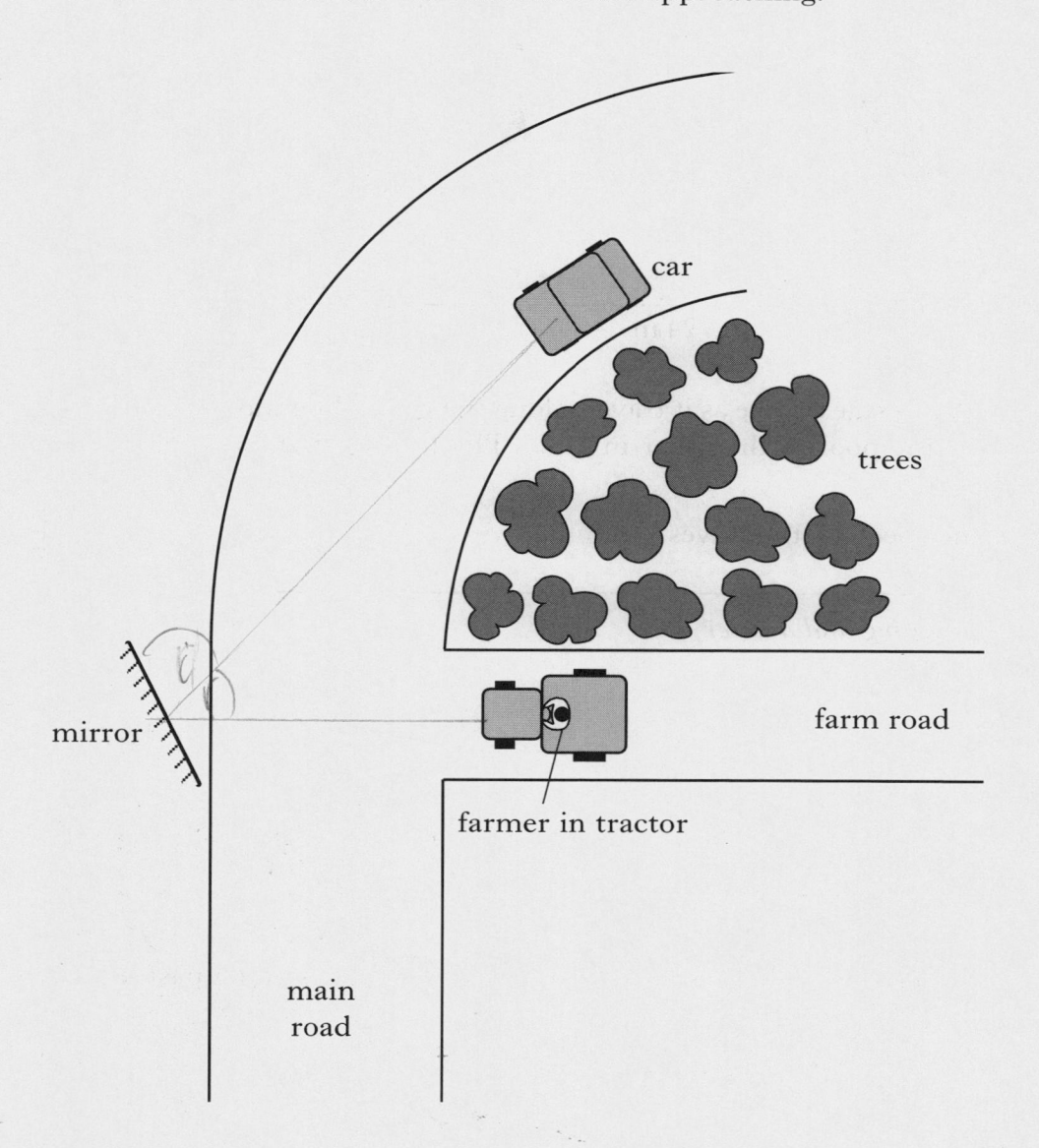

(a) On the diagram, draw rays to show how the farmer in the tractor can see the car by using the mirror.

You must label the angle of incidence and the angle of reflection on your completed diagram.

(b) State why the driver of the car can **also** see the tractor using the mirror.

the mirror can work in both ways

2. Two students watch the waves produced by a wave machine at a swimming pool.

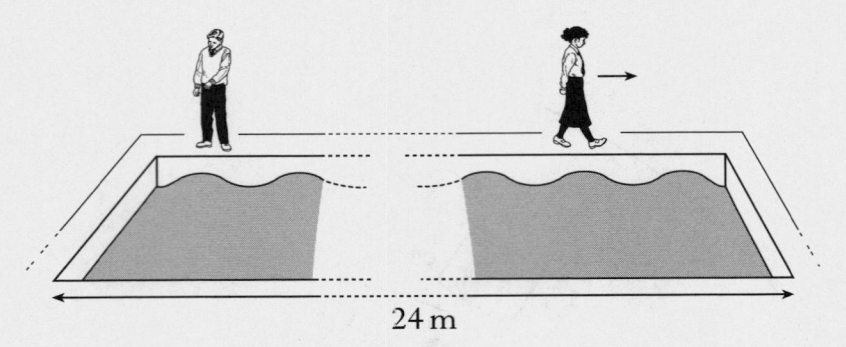

24 m

One student walks beside a wave as it travels along the pool. The wave goes from one end of the pool to the other in 20 s. The length of the pool is 24 m.

(a) Calculate the speed of the waves.

Space for working and answer

$s = d/t$
$s = 24/20$
$s = 1.2 \text{ ms}^{-1}$

(b) In the same time interval, the other student counts 5 waves going past the point where he is standing.

Calculate the frequency of the waves.

Space for working and answer

$f = v/\lambda$
$f = 1.2/4.8$
$f = 0.25 \text{ Hz}$

24/5
4.8

2. **(continued)**

(c) The students note that there are 5 complete waves in the pool at any time.

Calculate the wavelength of the waves.

Space for working and answer

$\lambda = v/f$
$\lambda = 1.2/0.25$
$\lambda = \underline{4.8 \, m}$

(d) Explain why "distance divided by time" and "frequency times wavelength" are equivalent for a wave.

Space for working and answer

$f \times \lambda$ = length of wave per second = $\dfrac{d}{t}$

[Turn over

3. A home entertainment centre consists of four appliances. The table gives the power rating of each appliance.

Appliance	Power rating (W)
television	110
video recorder	22
satellite receiver	20
DVD player	18

To operate properly, each appliance must be connected to mains voltage. The appliances are connected to the mains using a multiway adaptor.

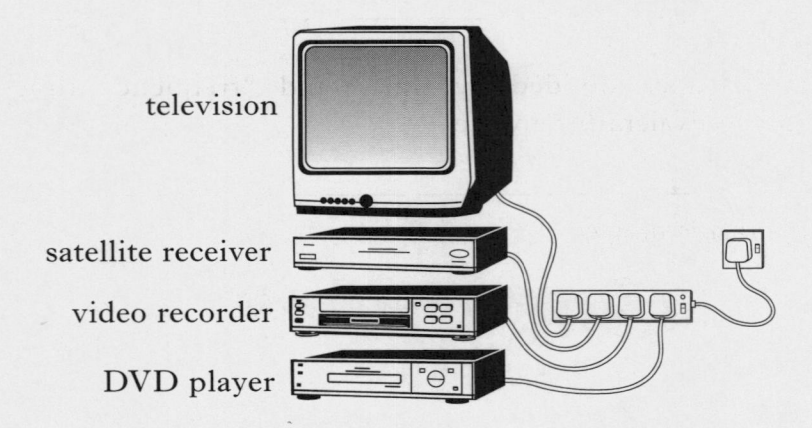

(a) (i) State the value of the operating voltage of the appliances.

230 V

(ii) The connections in the multiway adaptor are arranged to ensure that each appliance is connected to mains voltage.

State how the connections in the multiway adaptor are arranged to achieve this.

they are parallel

(b) Calculate the current from the mains when all four appliances are operating at the power ratings shown in the table.

(You must use an appropriate number of significant figures in your answer to this question.)

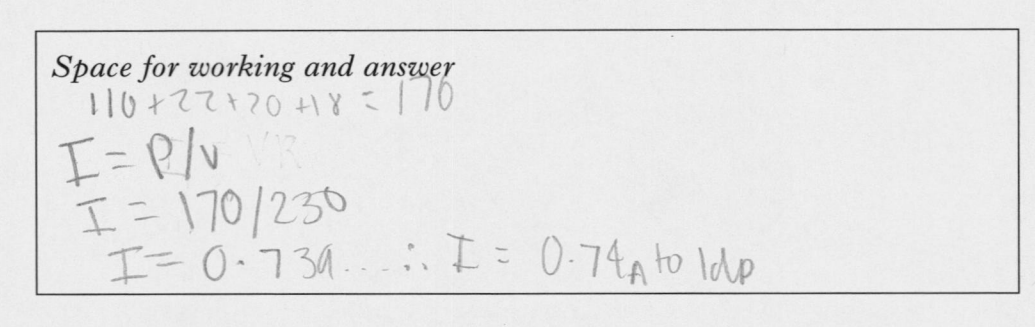

Space for working and answer

110 + 22 + 20 + 18 = 170

$I = P/V$

$I = 170/230$

$I = 0.739...$ ∴ $I = 0.74$ A to 1 dp

3. (continued)

(c) Calculate the resistance of the television when it is operating at the power rating stated in the table.

Space for working and answer

$V = IR$
$R = V/I$
$R = 230/0.74$
$R = 310.810...$
$R = 310.8 \, \Omega$

(d) The plug on the flex of the multiway adaptor contains a fuse.
What is the purpose of this fuse?

to protect the flex by melting the wires when too large a current is drawn

[Turn over

4. A show uses five spotlights of equal brightness, pointing at the same place on the stage.

The spotlights can be turned on and off individually. The colour of light from each spotlight is shown in the table.

Spotlight	Colour
1	green
2	blue
3	red
4	blue
5	green

(a) State **three** spotlights that could be on to produce white light on the stage.

1 (green) + 2 (blue) + 3 (red)

(b) One scene requires yellow light.

State **two** spotlights that could be on to produce yellow light on the stage.

1 (green) + 3 (red)

(c) Another scene requires **pale** green light. This needs **four** of the spotlights to be on.

State **one** spotlight that could be **off** so that the other four produce pale green light.

4 (blue)

5. A textbook has three diagrams showing how an eye lens changes when looking at objects that are different distances away. The diagrams below are copies of these three diagrams, with parts omitted.

Diagrams 1 and 3 are not complete.

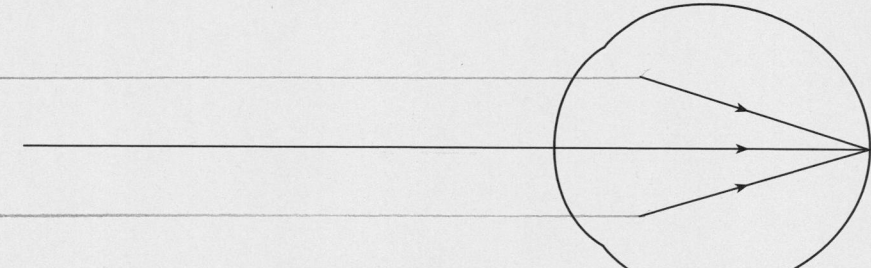

Diagram 1   looking at a boat on the horizon

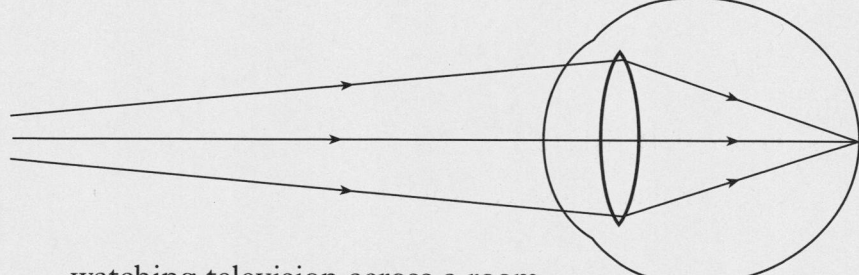

Diagram 2   watching television across a room

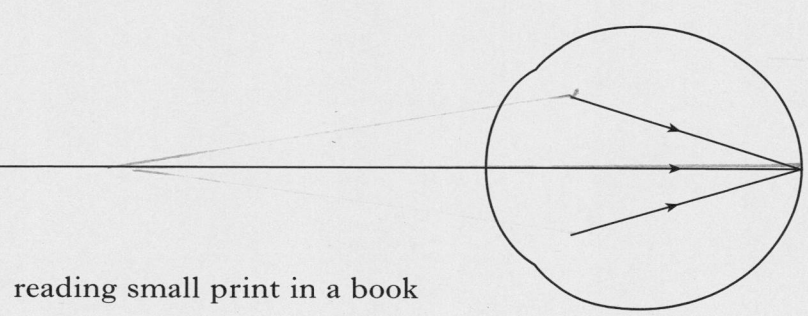

Diagram 3   reading small print in a book

(a) On diagrams 1 **and** 3:

  (i) draw two rays to show light coming from each object to the eye;

  (ii) draw a lens to show how the shape of the eye lens is different from the shape of the lens in diagram 2.

(b) The focal length of an eye lens system (the cornea and the eye lens together) is 2·5 cm.

Calculate the power of this eye lens system.

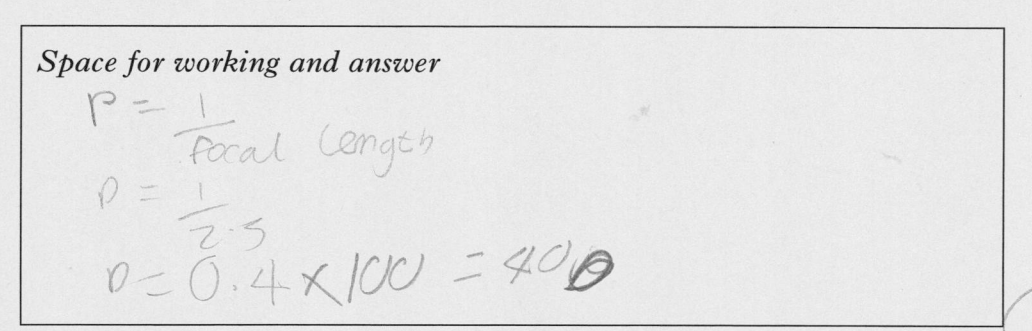

Space for working and answer

$P = \dfrac{1}{\text{Focal length}}$

$P = \dfrac{1}{2.5}$

$P = 0.4 \times 100 = 40$

6. A student designs the circuit shown to operate a 12 V, 3 A lamp from a 36 V supply.

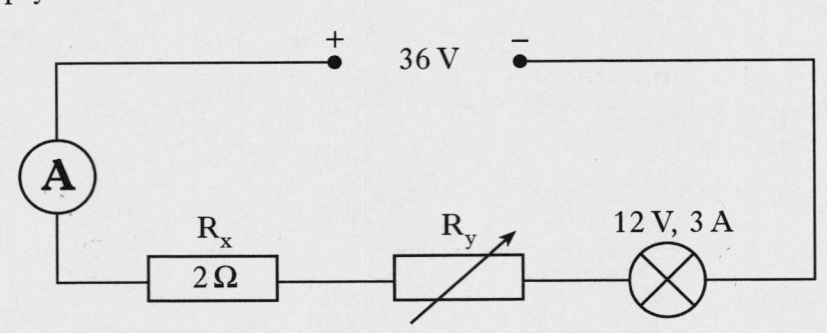

(a) What is the reading on the ammeter when the lamp is operating at its correct power rating?

...... 3 A ......

(b) The resistance of R_x is 2 Ω.

Calculate the voltage across R_x when the lamp is operating correctly.

Space for working and answer

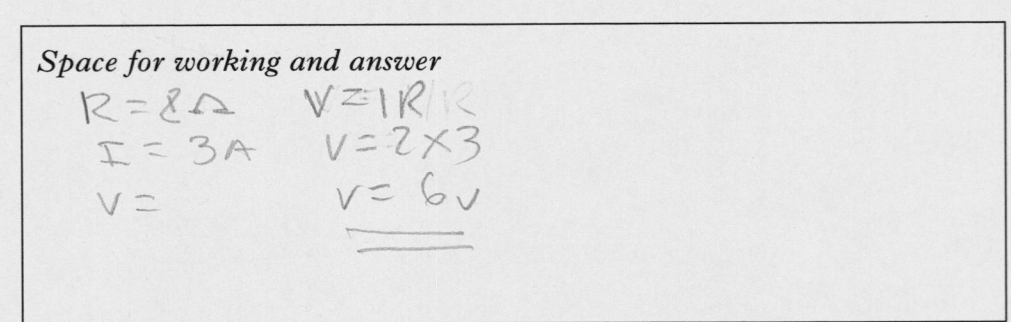

R = 2 Ω   V = IR
I = 3 A   V = 2 × 3
V =   V = 6 V

(c) Calculate the resistance of R_y when the lamp is operating correctly.

Space for working and answer

6. (continued)

(d) The student connects a second, identical lamp as shown in the diagram below.

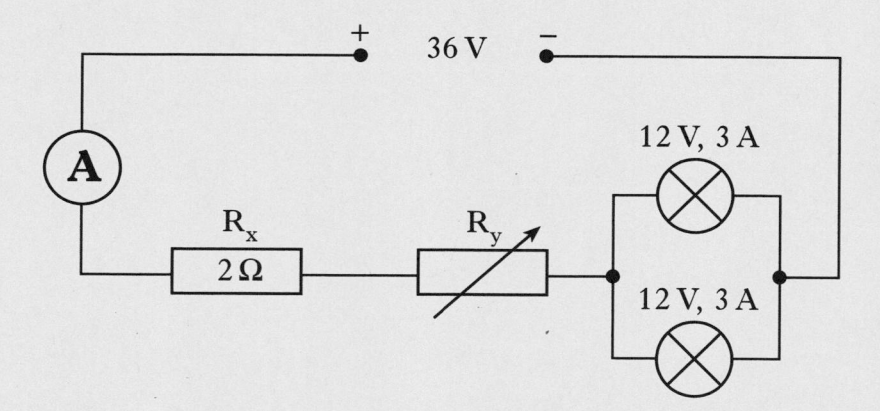

Explain why the resistance of R_y has to be adjusted for both lamps to operate correctly.

....

....

....

[Turn over

7. A paper mill uses a radioactive source in a system to monitor the thickness of paper.

(a) What is meant by the term "half-life"?

time taken for radioactivity to decrease

(b) The following radioactive sources are available.

Source	Half-life	Radiation emitted
P	500 years	alpha
Q	20 hours	beta
R	450 years	beta
S	300 years	gamma

(i) Explain why source P cannot be used in this system.

alpha would absorbed by paper

(ii) Which source should be used? Explain your answer.

7. (continued)

(c) Why does the radioactive source in the paper mill have a metal shield?

....

.... 1

(d) Another radioactive source emits gamma radiation. The graph shows how the activity of this source decreases with time.

activity in MBq vs time in hours graph, starting at 1600 MBq at 0 hours and decaying.

Calculate the half-life of this radioactive source.

Space for working and answer

1

8. A bus is fitted with a buzzer that sounds only when the bus is reversing. Part of the circuit that operates the buzzer is shown.

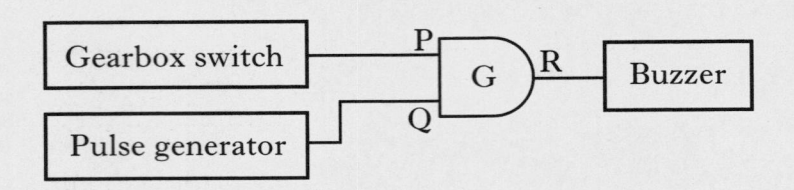

(a) Name logic gate G.

...........PROCESS.. 1

(b) The table shows the different possible combinations of logic levels (0 or 1) for input P and input Q to gate G.

Complete the last column of the table by **drawing** the output R from gate G for each combination of inputs.

Input P	Input Q	Output R
1 / 0	1 / 0	1 / 0
1 / 0	1 / 0 (pulses)	1 / 0
1 / 0	1 / 0	1 / 0
1 / 0	1 / 0 (pulses)	1 / 0

2

(c) The pulse generator part of the circuit is shown below.
The power supply to the NOT gate has been omitted for clarity.

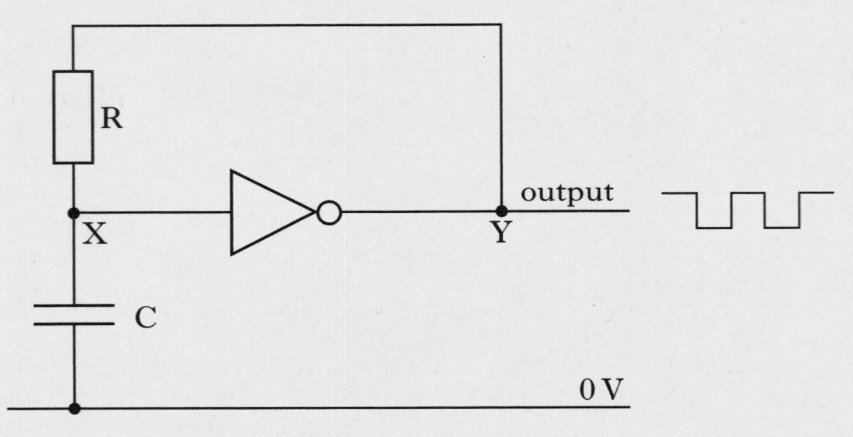

8. (c) (continued)

(i) Capacitor C is initially discharged.

Explain the operation of the pulse generator circuit, by referring to points X and Y in the circuit.

....

....

....

....

(ii) The pulse generator produces an output with a high frequency.

State **one** change that could be made to the circuit to give an output of lower frequency.

....

....

[Turn over

9. An electronic circuit is shown below. Component R is a thermistor.

(a) Name component P.

...... Variable resister 1

(b) (i) Name component Q.

...... transister 1

(ii) **In this circuit**, what is the function of component Q?

...... to allow the LED to light 1

(c) Explain how the circuit operates.

....

....

....

....

.... 2

10. A cyclist starts a journey in first gear and uses two other gears during the journey. After a short time the cyclist is forced to brake sharply and comes to a halt. A speed-time graph of the journey is shown.

At point P the cyclist changes from first gear to second gear.
At point Q the cyclist changes from second gear to third gear.

(a) (i) Before braking, which gear is the cyclist using when the acceleration is greatest?

third

(ii) Which gear does the cyclist use for the shortest time?

second

(b) Calculate how far the cyclist travels in second gear.

Space for working and answer

(c) Calculate the deceleration.

Space for working and answer

11. A model motor boat of mass 4 kg is initially at rest on a pond. The boat's motor, which provides a constant force of 5 N, is switched on. As the boat accelerates, the force of friction acting on it increases. A graph of the force of friction acting on the boat against time is shown.

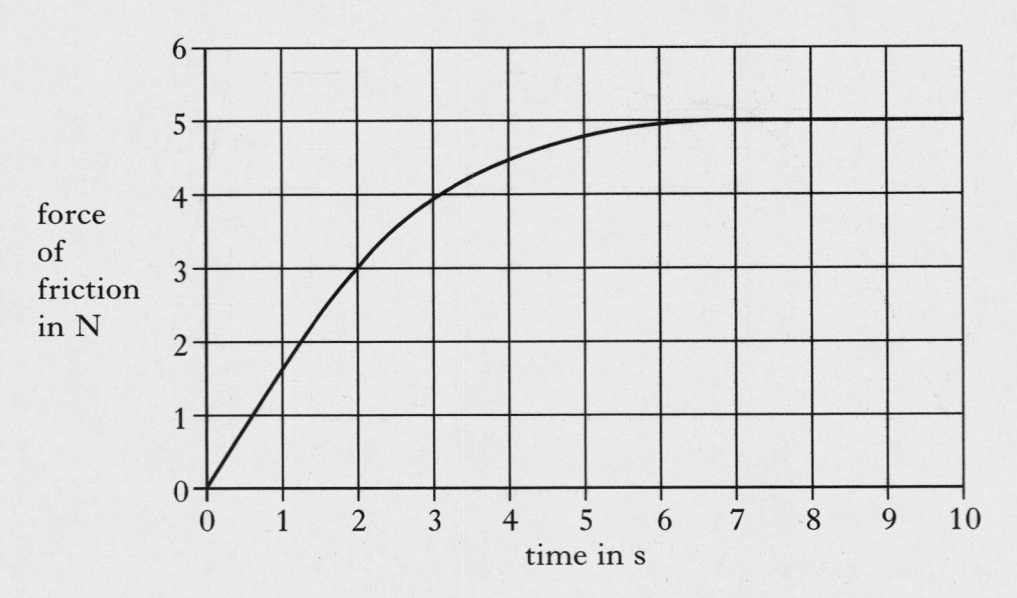

(a) (i) State the force of friction acting on the boat 2 s after the motor is switched on.

....3N..

(ii) Calculate the acceleration of the boat at this time.

Space for working and answer

$a = ?$ $a = fm$
$f = 3N$ $a = 4 \times 3$
$m = 4 kg$ $a = 12 ms^{-2}$

(b) Describe and explain the movement of the boat after 7 s.

After 7s the boat is moving at constant speed

12. A battery charger with an input voltage of 230 V is used to recharge a car battery. The charger contains a transformer that has an output voltage of 13·8 V.

(a) What type of transformer does the battery charger contain?

....

(b) There are 4000 turns in the primary coil of the transformer.

Assuming the transformer is 100% efficient, calculate the number of turns in the secondary coil.

Space for working and answer

(c) (i) When charging the battery, the current in the secondary coil is 4·7 A.

(A) Calculate the power output of the transformer.

Space for working and answer

(B) In practice, the transformer is only 94% efficient.
Calculate the current in the primary coil.

Space for working and answer

(ii) State and explain **one** reason why a transformer is not 100% efficient.

....

....

....

13. Water from a stream is used to drive a water wheel. The stream provides 6000 kg of water per minute to the wheel. The water falls a vertical height of 5 m.

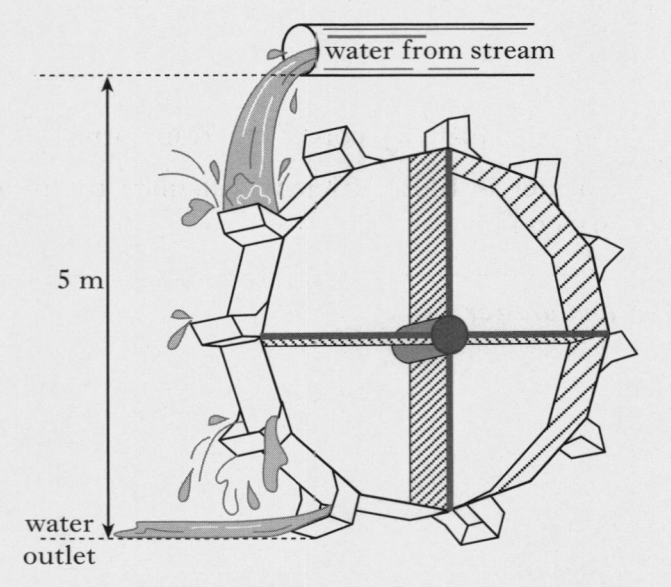

(a) Show that the maximum power available to the wheel from the water is 5000 W.

Space for working and answer

(b) The water wheel turns an electrical generator. The generator produces an output of 2990 W.

   (i) Calculate the efficiency of the water wheel and generator system.

Space for working and answer

13. (b) (continued)

(ii) Give **two** reasons why the efficiency of this system is not 100%.

....

....

....

....

(iii) The generator is connected to a heater in a shed. The heater heats the air in the shed. The mass of air in the shed is 161 kg. The specific heat capacity of air is 1000 J/kg °C.

Calculate the minimum time to increase the temperature of the air in the shed by 13 °C.

Space for working and answer

(iv) Give **one** reason why the actual time taken to increase the temperature of the air in the shed is greater than the value calculated in (iii).

....

....

[Turn over

14. Gamma rays, ultraviolet and infrared are three members of a family of waves. Every member of this family travels at the speed of light.

(a) What name is given to this family of waves?

.... microwaves ....

(b) Some uses of waves in this family are shown below.

Photographing bones inside a body

Tanning with a sun-ray lamp

Sterilising medical instruments

Communicating with mobile phones

Linking networked computers through optical fibres

Treating injuries using a heat-lamp

(i) From the examples above, give a use for:

gamma rays ....

ultraviolet ... tanning with a sun-ray lamp ...

infrared ... treating injuries using a heat lamp ...

(ii) Which of the three waves in (i) has:

the longest wavelength ... ultraviolet ...

the highest frequency? ....

15. A darts player throws a dart horizontally at the centre of the inner bull. The dart leaves the player's hand at a distance of 2·16 m from the dartboard and with a horizontal speed of 12·0 m/s.

(a) Calculate the time taken for the dart to travel from the hand to the board.

Space for working and answer

(b) Explain why the dart follows a curved path in its flight to the board.

....

....

....

(c) The average vertical speed of the dart during its flight to the board is 0·9 m/s.

How far below the centre of the inner bull does the dart hit the board?

Space for working and answer

[END OF QUESTION PAPER]

YOU MAY USE THE SPACE ON THIS PAGE TO REWRITE ANY ANSWER YOU HAVE DECIDED TO CHANGE IN THE MAIN PART OF THE ANSWER BOOKLET. TAKE CARE TO WRITE IN CAREFULLY THE APPROPRIATE QUESTION NUMBER.